The
Armies and Uniforms
of Marlborough's Wars

by

CS Grant

Colour illustrations by Bob Marrion

PARTIZAN PRESS

Published by Partizan Press 2004
816 - 818 London Road, Leigh-on-sea,
Essex, SS9 3NH
Ph/Fx: +44 (0) 1702 473986
Email: ask@caliverbooks.com
www.caliverbooks.com

First published in Great Britain in 2004 by Partizan Press

All colour illustrations except the two of Irish Regiment in
French service by H Boisselier are the work of Bob Marrion.

Design & Production by Jay Forster (www.generate.me.uk)

ISBN: 1-85818-506-8

Printed in the UK by FLPS

Front Page:
A soldier of Colonel Wynn's Regiment by Bob Marrion
© *Bob Marrion 2004*

Previous Page:
French infantryman. (*After Antoine Watteau*)

OTHER PARTIZAN HISTORICAL TITLES:

1 The Origins and Development of Military Tartans
James D Scarlett

2 The Last Scots Army 1661-1714
Stuart Reid

Coming Soon

4 Russian Opolchenie of the Napoleonic Wars
Dr S Summerfield

5 British Cavalry in the C18th
David Blackmore

Partizan Special Edition series:
1 Sieges and Fortifications of the Civil Wars in Britain
Mike Osborne

Partizan Army Guides series:
1 The Organization of the Texan Army
Stuart Reid

CONTENTS

FORWARD

My interest in the Marlburian period stemming from my childhood, inspired like so many other things by my late father, led me in the early 80's to sit down and conduct some serious research on the period. This was in large part captured in the now out of print "From Pike to Shot" published in 1986. Over the years I have returned to the subject, updating bits of the work as the publication of additional sources increased the information available.

I was therefore delighted, in this the tercentenary of Marlborough's victory at Blenheim, to be asked by David Ryan of Caliver Books to update my work for a new book. If the end result is half as rewarding for the reader as it has been for the author I will be very satisfied.

As a point of clarification, although it was only with the Act of Union in 1707 that the term British came into use, I have used it here prior to that date, rather than more accurately to refer to the English, Scots and Irish armies (unless I wished to differentiate) each of which had its own establishment prior to the Act of Union.

I would like to pay special tribute and thanks to Stuart Asquith who volunteered to read the manuscripts and, as ever, provide me with great support, encouragement and advice. Any errors that remain are entirely my responsibility. I am also greatly indebted to Bob Marrion who has allowed me to reproduce his colour artwork without reward other than the normally courtesies of acknowledgement. I am indeed honoured to have his superb colour illustrations to supplement my basic line drawings. I am very grateful to Dave Ryan for providing me with the opportunity to reawaken an old interest and again share my love of this subject with others. Finally my thanks to my son Charles, whose wizardry with the camera was essential and to my wife, Liz, who helped with the seemingly endless tables and with her encouragement.

C S GRANT
Farkhill
2004

BACKGROUND TO THE
WAR OF THE SPANISH SUCCESSION

The War of the Spanish Succession covered the period 1701 to 1714, but its roots lay in the previous century. By the end of the 17th century the vexed political subject of who should succeed Charles II, the Spanish Hapsburg King of Spain, had haunted Europe for more than a quarter of a century. Charles II was childless and consequently there were claimants for the throne in several of the European royal houses. The problem arose from the size, position and wealth of the Spanish empire - if this were added to one of the other major royal houses, or came under direct influence it would make the house extremely powerful and the political power centre of Europe. The Austrian Empire and France were the prime contenders for the throne. Their candidates were the Archduke Charles and the Duke of Anjou respectively, while a third was the Electoral Prince Joseph Ferdinand of Bavaria.

The Partition Treaty of 1698 made some attempt to solve this problem but agreement between the powers collapsed. Spain now declared for the Electoral Prince and this went into Charles II's will. Almost immediately the young heir to this huge estate died. A second partition treaty followed but was not accepted by Austria. Other machinations ended with the King leaving his throne to the Duke of Anjou in October and dying shortly afterwards in November 1700. Louis XIV proclaimed Philip of Anjou, Philip V, King of Spain. Henceforth Spain would be a French pawn.

It was another year before the full implications of these actions were to precipitate war. The final act was the French occupation of the fortress barriers of the Spanish Netherlands in February 1701. This act was accomplished without bloodshed and with the assistance of the Spanish garrisons, previously the Dutch allies. Although William III was nearing his end he appointed John Churchill, Earl of Marlborough and Captain General of the Forces, as Commander in Chief of Britain's forces in Holland. Marlborough departed for Europe and by meeting and diplomacy began to build the Grand Alliance between England, Holland, Austria, Prussia, Portugal, Denmark and a number of German states. France was already allied with Spain as well as Savoy (although Savoy soon joined the Grand Alliance), Mantua, Cologne and in 1702, after some treacherous double dealing, Bavaria. Such then was the background to a period of European warfare that lasted more than 10 years.

CHRONOLOGY OF THE MARLBURIAN WARS

This chronology deals principally with the events surrounding Marlborough in the Low Countries and the area of the River Danube. Only brief mention is made of other major battles in other theatres.

1700
- Duke of Anjou succeeded to the Spanish throne.

1701
- **February:** France occupied the Dutch held frontier fortresses in the Spanish Netherlands and England, Holland and the Hapsburg Empire prepared for war.
- **June:** The Earl of Marlborough was appointed Captain-General of the English Army and Ambassador Extraordinary to the Dutch Republic.
- **September 7th:** The Grand Alliance formed against the French King Louis XIV and signed in the Hague.

1702
- **March:** Queen Anne succeeded William III in England.
- **May:** Grand Alliance declared war on France.
- **June:** Marlborough recognised as Allied Generalissimo by Dutch.
- Marlborough attempted to bring the Duc de Boufflers into battle but failed, in part due to the constraints of the Dutch Deputies with the allied army.
- **September - October:** Marlborough captured fortified towns and cities of Venloo, Ruremonde and Liege.
- Also in this year, on the Rhine, Prince Louis, Margrave of Baden, with an Imperial army, captured Landau and moved to threaten Alsace. The Bavarian army however, seized Ulm and changed sides declaring war on the alliance. This forced Prince Louis to bring his army back over the Rhine to protect his own country thus relieving the pressure on the French. In October Prince Louis' army was defeated by Marshal Villars at Friedlingen.

1703
The campaigns in Low Countries including the siege of Bonn and the battle of Erckeren. Marlborough took Cologne and Bonn in May but was unable to take Antwerp. His operations were restricted by the Dutch Deputies with whom he had to work.

1704
To assist Austria, Marlborough was able to in part fool the Dutch Deputies and in an amazing feat of logistics and strategy, moved his army from the Low Countries to the Danube. Marlborough realised the need to support Austria by relieving the pressure on Vienna, but knowing the Dutch would not agree, deceived the latter into believing he was going to operate in the Moselle area. Instead he marched to the Danube.
- **May 19th:** Marlborough's army began its march from Low Countries to join the Austrians on the Danube. Here he was able to join up with the Austrians and Louis of Baden.
- **July 2nd:** The Allies successfully stormed the Franco-Bavarian position in the Schellenberg at Donauworth defeating the Bavarians in the process. In an attempt to draw the Franco-Bavarian army into a further battle Marlborough then ravaged Bavaria.
- **August 13th:** The Battle of Blenheim. The united French and Bavarian armies under Marshal Tallard were attacked at Blenheim and defeated by the Duke of Marlborough and Prince Eugene.
- In the final months of the campaign Marlborough took Landau, Trier and Trauback before returning with his army to the Low Countries.
- **November-December:** Marlborough's army returned to the Low Countries.

1705

- **May:** The Allied campaign began in the Low Countries. Marlborough wished to invade France through the Moselle region but this was too ambitious for the Dutch. Instead he manoeuvred in Flanders but once again his own allies caused him to forfeit battle when the circumstances were good. Little was gained in the year.
- **July 17-18th:** Marlborough forced the lines of Brabant. Battle of Elixem.
- **September:** Lord Peterborough headed the expedition to Spain.

1706

Once again Marlborough was forced to campaign in the Low Countries. Marshal Villeroi, attempting to shield the allied move on Namur came to battle at Ramillies.
- **May 23rd:** The Battle of Ramillies. Marlborough completely defeated the French and pursued them.
- **June-October:** During the remainder of the campaign the allies retook much of the Spanish Netherlands as Villeroi lost the line of the River Scheldt, Ghent, Bruges, Antwerp and Ostend. Menin, Dendermond and Ath followed this. Marshal Vendome was moved from Italy to replace Villeroi.
- Allies in Spain capture Valencia and Madrid, but forced to withdraw.

1707

- **May - August:** The allied activity in the Low Countries was hampered firstly by the Dutch reluctance to risk combat and later by the bad weather. The latter reduced the roads to a quagmire and made movement impossible. The year's campaigning was fruitless
- **April 25th:** The allies under General Galway in Spain were defeated at Almanza with a part of the army surrendering.

1708

- **June:** French in Flanders advanced north from Mons. Taking the initiative the French retook Bruges and Ghent, which were betrayed into their hands. They then laid siege to Oudenarde.
- **July 11th:** The Battle of Oudenarde. Marlborough and Prince Eugene defeat the Duke of Burgundy and Marshal Vendôme. The French were soundly defeated, but Vendome rallied his forces the next day and was able to halt the allies' pursuit at Ghent.
- **August:** Marlborough and Prince Eugene began the siege of Lille.
- **September 28th:** In September the allies were running short of supplies. An attempt by the French to prevent a major supply convoy from Ostend reaching the Allied besieging forces was foiled by the action of Wynedael.
- **December 9th:** Marshal Boufflers surrendered at Lille.
  Allies captured Sardinia and Minorca.

1709

- The previous year's campaigning only ceased after Marlborough took Bruges and Ghent.
- The French remained on defensive in the Low Countries.
- **July-September:** Marlborough besieged and captures Tournai and advances on Mons. Villars had been ordered by the King that if necessary to fight a general battle to hold Mons. The French army deployed and dug in in the area of Malplaquet, threatening the allied siege.
- **11 September:** Battle of Malplaquet. Marlborough and Prince Eugene defeat Marshals Villars and Boufflers, but at heavy cost.
- **October:** Capture of Mons.
- The Allies were defeated in Portugal in April at Val Gudina. After a breakdown in negotiations stalemate followed.

1710

- **April-November:** Marlborough besieged French frontier fortresses on Rivers Lys and Scarpe.
- **Winter:** Douai and Bethune fell to the allies after siege in June and August respectively. The remainder of the year was largely frustrating for Marlborough and inconclusive for the allies. In the winter months Villars began to build a set of defensive lines from Namur, through Arras to the coast. These were the lines of *Ne Plus Ultra*.
- In Spain, early allied successes at Almenara, Lerida and Saragossa were followed by reverses at Brihuega and Villaviciosa.

1711

By a campaign of deception and strategy, Marlborough was able to break the lines of *Ne Plus Ultra* on 5th August. In that month he laid siege to Bouchain, which fell to him on 14th September. Meanwhile, the Emperor of Austria had died and Charles, King of Spain and Hapsburg Emperor was unacceptable to the Alliance which started to collapse. Meanwhile intrigue, domestic pressures and conspiracy led to the dismissal of Marlborough who was recalled to England on 31st December.

1712

- In January the Duke of Ormonde took over command of the allied army. Eugene was keen to follow up Marlborough's gains of the previous year. However the government in Britain had changed.
- In May, quite contrary to the Grand Alliance, but as a result of secret negotiations between Britain and France, the Secretary of State (Henry St John, Viscount Bolingbroke) sent a secret restraining order to Ormonde. This ordered him not to participate with British forces in any siege or battle, neither were the allies to be informed of this decision. The French on the other hand were informed. Eugene learnt of the restraining order and many of the 50,000 European troops in English pay refused to obey Ormonde and stayed with Eugene. Eugene took Quesnoy after siege in July.
- **July 24th:** Eugene defeated at the battle of Denain. At the end of the month Villars deceived Eugene as to his intentions, fell upon and nearly destroyed the Dutch army, which in part due to the withdrawal of English pontoons could not escape.
- **October:** England began peace negotiations with France.

1713

- **April 11th:** Peace of Utrecht.

1714

- **September 7th:** Duke of Berwick took Barcelona. Austria and the Empire concluded the Treaty of Baden with France.

AN INTRODUCTION TO WARFARE
IN THE MARLBURIAN ERA

BACKGROUND

In order to understand the nature of warfare in the age of Marlborough it is necessary to see what preceded it in the latter part of the 17th century. The 17th century arguably saw the greatest changes in warfare since the introduction of the stirrup. It witnessed the rise of the standing armies, the proliferation and expansion of those armies, the domination of firearms and the development of drills and uniformity. All these aspects came together at the end of the century with the demise of the pike and the start of what might be called the horse and musket period of warfare, which was to extend to the American Civil War. The Marlburian period offers a fascinating study of the introduction of this period of warfare, which lasted over 150 years.

WEAPONS AND EQUIPMENT

The Pike

In the 1680s, the pike was still viewed as essential for the defence of the foot soldier against horse but its days were numbered. The development of a successful bayonet would provide the musketeer with his own means of self-defence rather than needing to rely on pike men. The gradual development of firepower for the foot soldier in the 17th century was changing the role of the infantry from shock action with the pike, to firepower with the musket and this change was directly reflected in the changing ratio of pike to musket. In 1600 there were generally five pikes to one musket, in the 1640s one pike to two muskets and by 1685 probably one pike to five muskets. The pike was an unwieldy weapon, which made any sort of movement in a formed body difficult and slow. By 1700 the pike had been almost completely withdrawn from the foot with the exception of the half pike, which was retained as a badge of rank and authority by officers and sergeants and to guard the colours of the regiment. The last users of the pike were the Swiss Guard in French service and the Spanish Army, both of which gave them up in 1703. There is also a record of the English 4th Foot handing in their pikes in 1702. Therefore, by the War of the Spanish Succession the pike had effectively disappeared from the battlefield. It should be noted that the transition in Eastern Europe was slower and the pike was still very much in evidence in the Great Northern War up to perhaps 1708.

The Musket

In the 1680's the normal musket was the matchlock. This was lighter then its predecessors and no longer required a forked rest for support. It was fired by a glowing slow match being lowered by means of a trigger into the pan containing priming powder. It remained a slow and inaccurate weapon with poor reliability. The slow match was a problem in the damp and its firer an easy target at night. The musket drills, with some 44 movements to reload, made it very slow; the rate of fire was probably about one shot per minute. It was effective to perhaps 250 yards, but it was wildly inaccurate and its operational range was more like 60 yards. By 1685, more effective muskets were becoming available. These replaced the slow match with the snaphance, which worked by means of a flint and hammer striking a plate, causing a spark that ignited the powder. These weapons, which developed into the flintlock, were lighter and simpler to use having only 26 movements to reload and which in theory could double the rate of fire. At the same time the calibre was smaller and 16

French officer after Rousselot

musket balls were produced to the pound, sometimes more, even up to 24. This was a great saving in weight on the matchlock with 12 balls to the pound and allowed more ammunition to be carried.

The introduction or more properly the conversion to flintlock was a slow one. In England the North British Fusiliers were given new weapons in 1678 but, apart from grenadier companies, it would seem that flintlocks were not generally issued until 1685. Apart from the Royal Regiment of Foot (later the Royal Scots) who we know had matchlocks at Sedgemoor (1685), some foot regiments had flintlocks. In Ireland in 1690 regiments had half matchlock and half flintlock. The French gradually introduced the fusil (a lighter type of firelock) so that there were eight per company in 1687 and 21 per company in 1692. Complete conversion was not achieved until about 1703. Lastly, it is worth illustrating the wide variety of firearms in the British army by noting that between 1687 and 1691 there were 14 varieties of musket in service. These included three matchlocks and four snaphances - uniformity in weapons was still a long way off. By 1700 most of the British foot had flintlocks, but the French were slower to change, waiting untill 1703 while the Austrians took even longer.

Ammunition

Along with the improvements in weapons came improvements in ammunition, specifically the pre-packed cartridge. Previously, musketeers carried a bandolier over the shoulder on which was suspended a dozen wooden cartridges, a bullet bag and a powder horn. The bandolier was often called "the twelve apostles" from the number of cartridges suspended from it. The bandolier gradually disappeared between 1670 and the 1690s. This was replaced by the cartridge pouch, which carried greased paper packages containing the necessary quantity of powder and the ball. The end of the cartridge was bitten off, the ball held in the mouth and the powder was tipped down the muzzle. The ball was then spat into the barrel and the paper used as wadding. This speeded the loading process. Like other developments the change was slow and probably not complete in the French army until 1738.

The Bayonet

In the 1680s the plug bayonet was in general service throughout Europe. This was a broad dagger with a round tapered handle, which was stuck into the muzzle of the musket. Whatever disadvantages the plug bayonet had, and there were many, it did provide the musketeer with a rudimentary pike. It therefore enabled him to use his firepower and to defend himself at close quarters. The disadvantages with this early bayonet were specifically associated with the plug design. Briefly, if musketeers had bayonets fitted from the outset of an action they might as well have had pikes. However, the fitting in action was so slow that if a volley was fired at about 60 paces the enemy were upon the firers before bayonets could be fitted. Once fitted it was virtually impossible to remove the plug bayonet in the heat of the battle in order to resume firing. The socket bayonet which first appeared in 1687 provided the answer to this problem. It replaced the plug bayonet and was introduced in to the English army and some German states in 1697 and in France in 1703. This design of bayonet permitted the musket to be fired by fitting the bayonet alongside or above the barrel of the weapon. It did nothing to improve the accuracy of the musket but it did give the user the opportunity to both fire and engage in close combat.

Side Arms

In the absence of a bayonet the sword had been the only means of self defence and hand to hand fighting for the infantry. The bayonet was not to change this for many years. All soldiers carried a sword of one sort or another. They were generally quite substantial weapons with blades of up to 30 inches long, with hilts and guards of brass. Side arms varied from country to country but were seldom standard within armies.

Bavarian Fusilier after Hoffman

The Grenade

The grenade dates from the mid 17th century. The weapon consisted of a hollow metal shell fitted with gunpowder and with a protruding match. Carried by grenadiers the grenade was a close quarter weapon used throughout Europe, but which gradually came to be used only in sieges. Grenadiers were established in many armies from the 1660s and by 1670 were frequently grouped into one company in a regiment. By the Marlburian Wars the grenadiers were used as elite companies and for specific tasks, for example in the storming of the Schellenburg, rather than the purpose from which their name arose.

Armour

Armour was still worn by the pikemen of most armies in 1685 and they would certainly have back and breast plates as well as a morion or pot helmet. In addition they might still have had some upper leg protection and a metal gauntlet. These had all disappeared with, and in some cases before, the pike. The horse or heavy cavalry generally wore back and breast plates over or under their coats although not by any means in all regiments. The transition began at this time from lobster helmets and triple barred or single bar face guard to soft brimmed hats with a metal crown either inside or outside the helmet.

TROOP TYPES

THE INFANTRY

One of the requirements and indeed the strengths of the pike had been the ability to fight in considerable depth, perhaps five or six ranks. By the start of the Marlburian Wars the pike had effectively disappeared, but the depth of a regiment at first remained unchanged.

Battalion Organisation and Strength

Battalion and company organisation was complex and varied from nation to nation and state to state. In order to provide some guidelines, the figures for France and England were:

- **France 1701:** Battalion of 690 men divided into one grenadier and 12 other companies each of 50 men.

- **England 1704:** Battalion of 750 men divided into one grenadier and 12 other companies of 57.

It is worthy of note that strengths could fluctuate greatly, whether in or out of war the difference between the official establishment and actual strength could be significant.

Infantry Firepower

With the demise of the pike the importance of firepower became paramount in infantry tactics. It was this feature that was to cause the gradual change in formation depth, specifically the number of ranks of musketeers. In 1685 musketeers fought five or six ranks deep, partly because the pike formations had been of this depth. The reduction in pikes and the desire to increase firepower resulted in changes to the firing drills.

Firing by Ranks. The first development to maximise the effect of the musket was the firing by ranks in volleys, but this was tied to the still dominant pike and it was a slow and ponderous system. Another reason was that this produced, at least in theory, a rolling system of fire. Initially, the front rank would advance three paces, fire and move to the rear and reload. The next rank would do the same and so on until the original front rank was at the front again. This provided one rank firing, three ranks ready and one reloading. This was called firing by rank. Two other methods in use were firing by "files" and by "divisions". In the former, two files (10 men) would deploy forward of the main body, form a rough line, fire and retire. In the latter system a division, consisting of four or six files, would carry out the same procedure. In both these examples it is quite clear that these methods were disruptive to the main formation, lacking in fire control and generally inefficient. They were the methods of 1685 but more efficient systems were being developed and these in turn would act to reduce the number of ranks and increase the available firepower.

Platoon Firing. The French remained conservative in their development of musketry fire, but this was not so elsewhere. The system of firing by platoons, perhaps having some foundation in the army of Gustavus Adolphus, was actually developed by the Dutch in the second half of the 17th century. The system was in turn adopted by the English in the War of the League of Augsberg, also called the Nine Years War. A battalion was subdivided for firing into four grand divisions, each of four platoons plus two platoons of grenadiers. The total of 18 platoons thus arrived at was divided into three firings each of six platoons. The battalion was deployed in three ranks, (on a frontage of 18 platoons), with each firing made up of six platoons distributed along the whole front. When ordered "First firing, take care", the whole of the front rank and the six platoons of the first firing made ready to fire. The front rank knelt and the second and third ranks locked with their bodies inclined to the right, right foot to the rear thus ensuring that the third rank had a clear field of fire. As soon as the first firing had taken place the first firing went into open order to reload and the second and third firings fired in turn. This method meant that the three rank system could produce a more effective fire over a broader frontage than the deeper formations, such as the firing by rank favoured by the French. An alternative to the three firings was to keep the front rank in reserve as a fourth firing.

Grenadiers

Grenadiers have already been mentioned. It remains to note that grenadiers were, from about 1670 onwards, organised by most countries as a separate company within a battalion. They had been generally the biggest and strongest soldiers best suited to throwing their grenades. Their characteristic headdress came into service by virtue of practicality. Broad brimmed hats common to the musketeers interfered with throwing the grenade. In addition to the grenade pouches, grenadiers also carried hatchets. The grenadiers were used in the field in their intended role in 1685 although the use of grenades was to be restricted more and more to siege warfare as the period continued. To the grenadier would fall the dangerous and demanding tasks and they were already recognised as the elite of the regiment and led the columns on the march.

THE CAVALRY

General

In the period between the end of the Thirty Years War and the Napoleonic Wars the proportion of cavalry to other arms in an army would drop quite dramatically in the armies of Europe. This had not yet started in this period and cavalry still comprised something in the order of 30% to 40% of an army.

Types of Cavalry

A wide ranging terminology was used to describe cavalry including horse, cuirassiers, dragoons, horse grenadiers, light horse and hussars. These too could be subdivided into elite, household and line troops.

Horse. The term "horse" is used to cover the heavy cavalry of the time and includes cuirassiers, carabineers and line heavy cavalry regiments. Cuirassiers were the traditional heavy cavalry and wore some armour depending on nationality. This could have been as much as back and breast plate (cuirass), iron gauntlets to the elbow and an iron lobster type helmet. The remaining "horse" were unarmoured but were otherwise equipped and used as cuirassiers. Carbineers were the same, but armed with the shorter carbine (that is

French cavalryman after Charles Parrocel

a short musket). Horse grenadiers were grouped in a troop or squadron and were as their name implies mounted grenadiers. Horse were armed with a brace of pistols, a carbine or musket and a long straight sword.

Dragoons. The dragoon in 1685 was very much a mounted infantryman, although this role would gradually change to favour their use as cavalry. Dragoons wore no armour and carried a carbine, bayonet, hatchet, broadsword and pistols. The dress was similar in style to the infantry although gaiters rather than boots were often worn. Dragoons in many armies wore low grenadier style hat. At this stage dragoons were a small percentage of the cavalry although this would increase over the next 50 years. They were the poor relations of the "horse", on lower pay and with poorer mounts.

Light Cavalry. The first regiments of hussars were introduced by Austria in 1688 and France in 1692 and at the start of the Marlburian Wars there were units in the Austrian, Bavarian and French armies. Their contribution to warfare in the first years of the 18th century was minimal and it was not until the time of Frederick the Great that the hussar found a proper place on the battlefield.

ARTILLERY

At the end of the 17th century the artillery was still in its infancy. In terms of organisation it was ad hoc and frequently only organised, as in the case of the English train, specifically for a campaign and then disbanded at the end. The artillery was usually organised not by those authorities responsible for the rest of the army, but by a separate authority. Such was the case in England with the Board of Ordnance and in France with the *Grand Maitre de L'Artillery* and his staff. In the early years the artillery was frequently grouped with, and was part of, the engineers. The artillery consisted of a mixture of permanent officers, regimental soldiers and civilian drivers. The artillery equipment of the period was a wide ranging mixture of old and new. In broad categories the equipment can be divided into cannons, mortars and howitzers. Cannon were deployed as both field and siege artillery, the mortar was a high trajectory weapon firing from a solid platform at a fixed angle, and the howitzer was a mobile and more versatile version of the mortar.

Artillery was first used for sieges but had been divided into siege and field artillery in the 17th century. In the 1690s the measure of calibre was translated into that of weight of shot, a process that started in the French army. These weights were 33,24,16,12,8 and 4 pounders, 12 and below being field artillery while the heavier calibres formed the siege train.

THE ENGINEERS

The engineers played an increasingly important part in 17th and 18th century warfare. One of the main reasons for this was the great importance attached to fortified towns and cities and the necessary sieges needed to take them. Despite this, the engineers at the time of Marlborough did not have the importance or status of other arms. They were, similar to the artillery, a very ad hoc organisation in European armies. They were generally an all officer corps, usually organised and coming under a separate agency from the rest of the army. In the case of England, this agency was the Board of Ordnance who also controlled the artillery. In war, the number of officers had to be increased and soldiers were drafted into the engineers from other units. In peacetime only a small number of officers remained on strength and these were employed inspecting, refurbishing and improving existing fortifications. The great engineers like Vauban and Coehoorn tried largely without success to put the engineers on to a more regular and effective footing. In 1685 a few of the more distinguished engineers would serve in an advisory capacity on a commander's staff. The junior officers would travel with and be part of the artillery train. Within the train there existed companies of miners and pioneers who assisted both the artillery and the engineers in their tasks. There would also be a bridging train of pontoons. This is only a brief synopsis of the engineer art and organisation as it stood at the turn of the 17th century. It can be seen that such divergent and important skills would quite understandably produce a requirement to place military engineering on a more formal, and structured basis. This was to be the theme for the next century.

TACTICAL PRACTICE

Finally, what follows is a brief historical description of the tactical practices of the period of the Marlburian Wars. Such a task is deserving of a book in itself and there is none better than David Chandler's "Art of Warfare in the Age of Marlborough" (see bibliography). This short section does not seek to repeat or even précis his work but simply to set out some elementary aspects of tactical practice.

Order Of Battle

The order of battle was a structured document setting out the deployment of the army in two or three lines. It was prepared well before the battle and therefore took no account of the ground, at least not initially. It provided the framework, which could then be modified as the ground and plan might dictate, for what was essentially linear warfare. Every unit would know its place and the identity of its neighbours. The total deployed frontage might be between two and three miles.
It was customary to divide the weight of the cavalry between the two flanks with perhaps a part kept centrally in reserve behind the two or three lines of infantry.

The artillery would be spread along the line grouped into batteries, however the concept of the grand battery had not yet appeared. The guns would move forward with the columns as they deployed into their line of battle and would deploy, perhaps slightly forward of the front line and seeking high ground which would provide a clear field of fire to support an advance. The artillery would be expected to move as far forward as the infantry line of battle, and the lighter battalion guns would keep pace with their parent units.

The era of the clash of pikes with densely packed bodies of men rushing together had gone to be replaced by firepower. One or both lines would advance to within 60 metres and engage in a firefight, which would test each other's resolve and determination. The artillery would support this. At the appropriate time one side would move forward to close with the enemy who might well not wait for the contact, but fall back or break. This is a gross simplification and within this the commander would be seeking the tactical advantage, deploying deception and cunning to unbalance his opponent. Authors disagree over the balance between the reliance of firepower and hand to hand action. The predominance of the former is certain, but there are good accounts that bear witness to the ferocity of the latter.

The horse, though not yet fully developed for "shock action" was becoming more widely used in this role. The role of the cavalry was quite simply to neutralise the enemy's cavalry. Anything more was a bonus for the commander.

Such was the basis upon which commanders of the period deployed their forces for battle. From such an apparently stereotyped procedure came some of the most varied and interesting battles of the 18th century.

SIEGE WARFARE

Siege warfare was an essential ingredient of the Marlburian wars. The science of fortifications, both in their construction, defence and besieging was a complex business that can only be briefly touched on here. The bibliography provides some references which cover this aspect of Marlburian warfare.

The Defence

The art of permanent defences reached their zenith in the mathematically precise constructions masterminded by the French engineer Vauban that were so much a feature of cities and towns of the Low Countries in the late 17th century. The structure of such fortifications was divided into a number of different elements. Each element contributed to the main purpose which, put simply, was to impede or prevent the approach of the enemy with a combination of obstacles and interlocking arcs of fire. The defence was based on a polygon with a number of protruding bastions linked by a curtain wall. In profile there would be a glacis, a palisade, covered way, counterscarp, a ditch, escarp, rampart, parapet, terreplein (a flat surface behind the parapet) and talus (interior slope of the rampart). The whole effect was to provide an angled front (glacis) swept by fire, behind which the sheltered defenders occupied the covered way. When this was in peril the defenders would withdraw back across the ditch to the ramparts from which they could again engage the assaulting enemy coming down the counterscarp into the ditch. The ditch was swept by fire from the bastions interlinked by fire from the troops on the curtain wall and in the ravelins and demi-lunes (individual defences within the ditch to link fire with the bastions).

The Attack

The length of a siege, while not entirely predictable, was usually a matter of following some fairly well understood procedures, which dictated that by and large the operation would be successful in between 40 and 60 days. The fortress would fall once two interlinked bastions were taken and the wall between was breached.

David Chandler quotes the following useful sequence:

To invest a place, collect material, and build lines	- 9 days
From the opening of the trenches to reaching the covered way	- 9 days
The storm and capture of the covered way and its defences	- 4 days
Descent into and crossing of the ditch of the demi-lune	- 3 days
Mining operations, siting batteries, creation of a fair breach	- 4 days
Capture and exploitation of the demi-lune and its defences	- 3 days
Crossing the main ditch to two bastions	- 4 days
Mining operations and siting of guns on the covered way to make a practicable breach	- 4 days
The capture of the breach and its supporting position	- 2days
Surrender of the town after the capitulation	- 2 days
Allowance for errors, damage caused by sorties, a valorous defence	- 4 days
Total	48 days

This outline description belies the enormous amount of work involved in the process. The investiture of a fortress would involve digging two lines of defences right around the objective beyond artillery range. These were the lines of circumvallation (outward facing to defend against the possible relief of the garrison from outside) and within it the line of contravallation (facing inwards). From the inner line communication zigzag trenches were dug forward to the first parallel. This was a line of defences following the same line as those of the fortress and along which artillery batteries were mounted. From this further communication trenches went forward to a second parallel and the batteries were pushed forward. The same procedure then followed to the third parallel from which the breach could be made and, if the fortress did not surrender, it could be stormed.

Artillery in action after CCP Lawson

The Forlorn Hope

The gradual progression of the siege, with its systematic and mathematical approach, to the point when the breach was made would frequently lead to the surrender or submission of the fortress without an assault. However, if capitulation did not come then an assault had to be made. The task fell to the "forlorn hope". This would be a force specifically appointed for the task, perhaps specially picked from volunteers, a detailed company or possibly grenadiers. To them fell the unenviable task and the glory of leading the final assault.

The forlorn hope or *enfants-perdus* (children without hope) was the name given to the storming party in an assault or, conversely, the rear party in a retreat. An 18th century military dictionary defines the "forlorn hope" in the following way:

> "Forlorn Hope - Signifies men detached from several regiments, or otherwise appointed to make the first attack in the day of battle: or at a siege, to form the counterscarp, mount the breach, &c. They are so called from the great danger they are unavoidably exposed to, but the expression is old, and begins to be obsolete"

Despite the last comment, the expression continued into the 19th century and the Napoleonic wars.

In the late 17th century the role was one that fell naturally to dragoons and grenadiers. David Chandler quotes from another military dictionary of 1702 on the role of dragoons in this respect:

> "Musketeers mounted, who serve sometimes a-foot and sometimes a-horseback, being always ready upon anything that requires expedition, as being able to keep pace with the horse, and do the service of foot. In battle, or upon attack, they are commonly the *enfants perdus*, or Forlorn [hope], being the first that fall on."

This role fell more naturally to the grenadier whose large stature, grenades (when they were used), and hatchet led them to be the normal choice for the forlorn hope, as they became the accepted elite of many armies. Quoting again from Chandler:

> "..the grenadiers were also called upon to form the nucleus of every "forlorn hope" storming party and every last-ditch garrison. One celebrated operation by a picked group of grenadiers took place at the siege of Lille (1708), when Sgt. Little succeeded in crossing the moat and hacking though the chains of a drawbridge immediately prior to the assault."

Logistics in Sieges.

Logistics played a major part in the whole process of sieges for both sides. The ability of the defender to endure the siege until it was broken by outside assistance depended on how well the fortress has been provisioned both with food, drink and ammunition. For the besieging force the enormous amount of stores, timber and artillery ammunition needed to sustain the siege was a major logistic consideration. The various sources quoted in the bibliography go into some detail on this matter. The battle of Wynendael arose as a result of a French attempt to prevent essential supplies reaching to Marlborough's besieging army at Lille.

French cavalryman after Charles Parrocel

THE AUSTRIAN ARMY

INTRODUCTION

Austria, centre of the Holy Roman Empire, was early to experiment in retaining armies in full pay throughout the year rather than just during the campaign season. These were however mercenary forces. Austria's first true standing army of regular soldiers was created in 1679. The architect of this army was Count Montecuccoli. As the president of the Hofkriegsrat between 1668 and 1681 he was able to lay the foundations of the Imperial Austrian Army. The Hofkriegsrat was a mixed civil-military organisation, which under the Crown, was responsible for organising the military affairs of the Empire. The task of forming an army was not an easy one. While those at the Court of the Empire were able to lead an extravagant life in considerable splendour the economy could never find enough funds to keep, equip and pay the army. The finances for the army came from estates, imperial diet and other revenues but these were never enough to cover the cost. Corruption also took a share of the available finances. Montecuccoli, while unable to greatly change the financial backing of the army, was able to make improvements in the command structure, training and technical development.

The army between 1679 and 1700 developed on much the same lines as other Western European armies. The flintlock musket gradually replaced the matchlock and the pike was replaced by the musket and bayonet. The army grew in both experience and size playing its part in the War of the Grand Alliance. Between 1697 and 1710 the army increased, from 29 to 40 regiments of foot, from seven to 20 cuirassier regiments, from one to 12 dragoon regiments and the introduction of five hussar regiments.

THE UNIFORMS

Details of specific Austrian uniforms are provided for a number of regiments in the separate table. The following notes are concerned with the generalities and the development of the uniform of the different arms.

The Infantry. Initially, the uniform of the infantry was a different colour for each regiment. The coats were very full and straight lined being untailored at the waist. Gradually grey became the predominant colour and in 1708 all infantry except the Dutch in the Austrian service were ordered to wear pearl grey. At the same time the coat became closer fitting, with large full cuffs, now tailored at the waist and full skirted to the knee. Each regiment was identified by the colour of the coat's lining and cuffs as well as the waistcoat, breeches and stockings. Officers, NCOs and musicians wore reversed colours, but it is likely that in the early 1700s the officers and NCOs gradually changed to the same colours as the rest of the regiment. It is not clear when the black and yellow or black and gold officers' sashes were introduced, but it may well have been at the same time. The hats followed the normal progression towards the tricorn, one side then all three being turned up, arriving there in the 1690s. Sprigs of greenery were worn in the hat as field signs to distinguish friend from foe. The grenadier hats were usually of fur, high fronted with a metal plate and a coloured bag to the side or rear. Another variation had a stiff fronted hat with bag and no fur. (See the Beyreuth Regiment in the table).

Cuirassier. Austrian cuirassiers wore a stout full skirted coat of buffer leather with full cuffs. They had stiff breeches, gauntlets and high boots. Over the coat was worn a black or silver front and back plate (cuirass) and at the throat was a coloured cravat. Both the tricorn and lobster tail helmet were worn, but the latter was retained in action unlike many countries that had ceased to use it.

A

B

C

17

D

Dragoons. The dragoons were dressed in coats of either red or blue. In place of the protection given by the cuirass they wore stiff leather jackets beneath the coat. Breeches were buff and high boots rather than gaiters were worn. The hat was a tricorn. They were equipped much as other dragoons with carbine hung from a shoulder belt, sword, bayonet and a pair of pistols. Horse grenadiers were introduced to the dragoons in 1711 and wore fur grenadier caps. There were also Spanish dragoons in Austrian service. These wore the characteristic Spanish dragoon hat with a high flat front curved at the top with a crown behind it. They too had horse grenadiers with fur hats. Otherwise they were dressed and equipped much as the other dragoons.

Hussars. The hussars stemmed from Austria being an ethnic troop type, indeed it is from Austria that the traditional hussar dress stemmed. At this stage the development of the hussar as a military arm was in its infancy and they probably did not have a uniform as such. The costume consisted of a fur hat with a cloth bag falling to one side. The coat was a tight fitting jacket, shortcut and fastened at the front with cords across the chest with buttons or toggles. Around the waist was a sash made of barrels like rope. A bag, the sabretache, hung from a string over one shoulder down onto the hip. Breeches, short boots and a curved sabre completed the dress. Ottenfeld's (see bibliography) Hussar, dated 1710, wears a brown fur cap with large red bag, dull olive green dolman (jacket) with dark green cords and cuffs, a red and olive green rope sash, white breeches and brown boots. The schabraque in red with an olive green saddle roll at the back.

E

F

Artillery. The Austrian gunners of the time were dressed much as the infantry. An illustration from Ottenfeld shows a gunner in coat, waistcoat, breeches and gaiters all in steel grey. The coat has dull red cuffs and the waistcoat is lined with the same colour. Buttons are yellow, the tricorn is black edged yellow and the figure wears a cravat. He carries a telescope suspended in a black case from the waist and holds an espontoon. In the background is a driver who is dressed in the same manner.

The Staff. General Officers dressed much as they pleased at this period. Prince Eugene wore a brown coat with gold lace and a black cuirass trimmed in red, and a black tricorn edged gold. His saddlecloth and pistol covers were red with gold lace and embroidery. Ottenfeld shows a general of 1720, in a red coat and waistcoat with gold lace. The figure wears a black cuirass under the open coat and over the waistcoat. Around the waist is a silver sash with gold threads. The breeches are white with big black boots. The hat was a black tricorn edged gold with a white trim. The saddlecloth and pistol caps are light blue with gold lace.

G

Illustrations

A	Foot	B	Foot grenadier 1710	C	Cuirassier 1705
D	Dragoon 1710	E	Hussar 1710	F	Artillery 1710
G	Cuirassier Officer 1700				

AUSTRIAN HORSE AND DRAGOONS

REGIMENT	Coat	Lining	Cuffs	W/coat	Breeches	Schabraque	Remarks
KUIRASSIERS						Red with trim as below	
Lothringen until 1705, Breuer	Leather/Buff	Red	Red	Leather/Buff	Red	Yellow, narrow red edge	Black cravat, yellow buttons
Visconti	Leather/Buff	Red	Red	Red	Red	White, Yellow edge	Red cravat
Taffee until 1704 then Leiningen, 1705 Reising, 1706 Pfefferkorn, 1707 Hautois	Leather/Buff	Red	Red	Leather/Buff	Leather/Buff	Blue and white triangle edge.	White cravat
Cusani	Leather/Buff	Dark Red	Dark Red	Dark Red	Red	Yellow edged red	Yellow buttons, white cravat
Jung Hannover	Leather/Buff	Red	Red	Red	Red	Yellow edged red	White cravat
Alt Hannover	Leather/Buff	Red	Red	Red	Red	Yellow/red/yellow	white buttons, white cravat, white edge on pocket
Uhlefeld	Buff	Red	Red		Red	White edged Red	White cravat
Roccavione	Leather/Buff	Dark Red	Dark Red	Dark Red	Dark Red	White edged Red	White cravat
Pfalz-Neuburg	Leather/Buff	Red	Red	Red	Red	Light blue edge with white diamonds	Cuff edged light blue, buttons copper, black cravat
Gronsfeld	Leather/Buff	Red	Red	Red	Red	Yellow edged Red	White cravat
Vaudemont	Buff	Red	Red	Red	Red	White and blue triangles, edged red	White Buttons, Red cravat
Commercy till 1702, Falkenstein	Leather/Buff	Bright Blue	Bright Blue	Red	Red	Yellow edged red	White buttons
Palffy	Leather/Buff	Red	Red	Red	Red	White/red/white	
Xanthe until 1704, Lobkowitz	Leather/Buff	Red	Red	Red	Red	Yellow braid with blue edge	White cravat
Darmstadt	Buff	Light Blue	Light Blue	Light Blue	Red	Yellow edged above and below in blue	Red cravat
Montecuccoli	Buff	Blue	Blue	Buff	Buff	Blue Schabraque. White and light blue triangles	White buttons, white cravat
Mercy	Leather/Buff	Red	Red	Red	Leather	White edged yellow	White cravat
DRAGOONS							
Rabutin	Blue	Red	Red	Blue	Buff	Red edged yellow, small red circles on to[and bottom edges	Lace white
Styrum until 1704, Sinzendirf until 1707, Vehlen	Red	Green	Green	Buff	Buff	Red edged yellow	Lace yellow
Savoyen	Red	Black	Black	Red	Buff	Red edged yellow	Lace yellow
Trautmannsdorf until 1706, Reising until 1711, St.Amour	Blue	Red	Red	Blue	Straw	Red edged yellow	Lave yellow
Castell until 1704, Palffy until 1706, von Batte	Light Blue	Carmine	Carmine	Carmine	Light Blue	Carmine, blue inner braid then carmine again then yellow	Lace yellow
Herbeville until 1709, Jorger	Red	Black	Black	Red	?	Red edged yellow with a narow blue centre stripe	Lace white
Schlick until 1705, Althann	Green	Red	Red	Red	Red	Red edged yellow	Lace yellow
Sereni until 1705, Fels	Yellow	Red	Red	Black	Buff	Red edged yellow	Lace white
Vaubonne	Blue	Red	Red	Blue	Buff	Red edged yellow with thin blue lines top and bottom	Lace yellow
Bayreuth	Light Blue	Carmine	Carmine	Carmine	Carmine	Carmine, Schabraque border yellow with light blue crosses	White buttons
Fels, 1705 Breuner	Blue	Red	Red	Blue	Straw	Red edged yellow with blue edges	Yellow buttons
Prinz Eugen	Red	Black	Black	Red	Leather /Buff	Red edged yellow	Gold edge on hat, gold buttons

AUSTRIAN FOOT

REGIMENT	Coat	Lining	Cuffs	W/coat	Breeches	Stockings	Remarks
Arnant	Pearl Grey	Scarlet	Scarlet	White	White	Scarlet	Hat edged white, copper buttons
Baden-Baden	Bright Blue	White	White	White	White	White	Hat edged white, white buttons
Bayreuth (Brandenburg - Bayreuth)	Bright Blue or Dark Blue	Carmine	Carmine	Carmine	Leather or White	Carmine	Hat edged white, small red collar, grenadier hat black fronted edged silver with gold grenade. Red/yellow bag.
Alt Daun, 1706 Gutenstein	Pearl Grey	Red	Red	Red	Red	Red	Hat edged white, white buttons
1698 Hasslingen	White	Carmine	Carmine	Carmine	Leather	Carmine	Hat edged white
Longueval, 1703 Koenigsegg	Pearl Grey	Bright Blue	Bright Blue	Bright blue	Bright Blue	Bright Blue	Hat edged white, white buttons.
1702 Chalons 1702 Alt Starhemberg	Pearl Grey	Blue	Blue	Blue	Leather/Buff	Grey	Hat edged white, yellow buttons.
Thuerhein	Pearl Grey. Red square lapels and red collar.	Red	Red	Pearl Grey	Pearl Grey	Pearl Grey	Red hackle in hat but no edging.
1700 Salm, 1704 Wallis	Pearl Grey	Bright Blue	Bright Blue	Bright Blue	Bright Blue	Bright Blue	Hat edged white.
Wendt	Pearl Grey	Red	Red	Red	Red	Red	Hat edged white, white buttons.
Fuerstemberg,1703 Longueval,1703 Wurttemberg	Light Grey		Light Grey	Red		White/Grey	Hat edged white, Grenadier hat, bag white lace
Walloon	Dark Green		Crimson	Crimson	Crimson	White	Seven regiments of Walloons in Austrian service.
1700 Palffy	Light Grey	Red	Red	StrawYellow	Straw Yellow	Red	Hat edged white
1701 Kriechbaum, 1710 Waachtendonk	Light Grey	Red		Red			
Bagni	Light Grey	Light Grey	Light Grey	White	Light Grey	White/Blue stripe	Hat edged white, Blue neck scarf
1696 Guttenstein 1706 Wetzen	Medium Blue	Pearl Grey	Pearl Grey	Pearl Grey	White	Grey	Hat edged white
1694 Thuengen, 1709 Holstein-Beck	Light Grey	Light Grey	Dark Blue?	Paille	Paille	White/Blue stripe	Hat edged white, Red neck scarf
Harrach	Grey	Grey	Dark Blue	Dark Blue	Dark Blue	Grey	Hat edged white, Red neck scarf, Grenadier bearskin with brass shield, dark blue bag edged yellow
Alt Heister Nigrelli 1703 zum Jungen	Green	Red	Dark Blue	Dark Blue	Dark Blue	Green	Hat edged white Bearskin brass shield dark blue nag with yellow border and ball.
Duke Salm	Bright Grey	Red	Red	Red	Red	Red	
Lorraine, 1705 Wetzel, 1706 Hoffman 1707 von Heindle-Sonnenburg	1706 White	Red	Red	Red	White		
Marsigli,1704 Joerger de Tollet	Bright Grey			Red	Red	Red	Hat edged white
Gschwind	Bright Grey	Red	Red		Leather	Bright Grey	Hat edged white
Daun, 1711 Alt Daun	Pearl Grey	Red	Red	Pearl Grey	Pearl Grey	Red	Red cockade on hat, Grenadiers bearskin with red red bag, Buttons yellow
Nehem	White/Grey	Blue	Blue	Light Leather	Light Leather		Hat edged white
Sickengen 1713 Wallenstein	Bright Grey	Black	Black	Bright Grey	Bright Grey		Hat edged white
Neipperg	White Grey	Blue	Blue	White/Grey	White/Grey		Hat edged white
Loeffelholz-Colberg	White	Red	Red	Red	Red	White	Hat edged white Red collar
Reventlau,1711 O'Dwyer	White/grey	Light Blue	Light Blue	White/Grey	White/Grey		
Hoch und Deutschmeister	White/grey Yellow buttons	Blue	Blue	Blue	Blue	White	Hat edged white
Lorraine	1701 Green 1708 Pearl Grey	Green Green	Green Green	Red Red	Green Green	White Red	Hat edged white
Saix d'Arnaut, 1702 Holstein-Ploen, 1704 Saix d'Arnaut	Light Grey	Light Red	Light Red	Light Grey	Light Grey	Light red	Hat edged white, Grenadier fur cap, red bag, yellow tassel
Von Diesbach	White/grey	Red	Red		White Grey		Hat edged white, Buttons yellow
Von Erlach	Pike Grey	Dark Blue	Dark Blue	Red			
Herberstein	Light Grey	Light Grey	Light Grey	Buff Leather	Buff Leather	Red	Hat edged white Buttons yellow

Austrian - Infantry Longueval
© Bob Marrion 2004

Austrian - Grenadier, Brandenburg - Bayreuth
© Bob Marrion 2004

Austrian - Cuirassier Regiment Cusani
© Bob Marrion 2004

Bavarian - Cuirassier Regiment Weickel c.1701

© Bob Marrion 2004

THE BAVARIAN ARMY

A

INTRODUCTION

The Bavarian army, like the army of other German States after the Treaty of Westphalia, grew slowly and almost surreptitiously. In 1664 it numbered 1,750 and by 1675 it had grown to the 8,000 men fought that with the allies in the Grand Alliance. In the War of the Spanish Succession Bavaria changed sides early on to fight on the side of the French. The Elector Max II Emanuel was somewhat enamoured of the French and Louis XIV and in consequence the Bavarian army from 1700 onwards had many of the French characteristics. The alliance was to cost Bavaria greatly in particular in the year of the Schellenburg and Blenheim.

B

Like many other European nations distinctive uniforms for the Bavarian army dated from this era, beginning in 1671; not surprisingly in fashion and cut they were similar to other armies.

UNIFORMS

The uniform detail, which specifically concerns the Bavarian army in the War of the Spanish Succession, is given by regiments in the separate table. The following information will serve to cover the broad trends and developments through the period.

The Foot. By 1700 all Bavarian infantry were wearing coats of sky blue with regimental distinctions. The coat was tailored at the waist, without collar but still with full cuffs, and cut several inches above the knee. This was worn with a waistcoat somewhat shorter than the coat, breeches and gaiters, which buttoned up the outside leg to above the knee. A stouter buckled shoe had appeared to replace a less suitable style. The tricorn was the standard headwear and the grenadiers wore the fur bonnet. The equipment included the sword and bayonet on a waist belt and the large cartridge pouch, almost one foot square, hanging from a shoulder belt. On campaign a water bottle, large fur covered bag and greatcoat would also be carried. On campaign a water bottle was suspended from a shoulder strap worn over the right shoulder. The pike had gone out of service, except for half pike carried by NCOs and officers, in the 1690. Drummers and fifers wore the same colour coats as the musketeers with white lace on the jacket and cuff buttons, seams and chevrons or hoops up the arms. The officers wore the same colour coats as the men, but the NCOs wore coats of the facing colour with sky blue cuffs.

D

C

Horse. In 1700 there were three cuirassier regiments plus the *Leibgarden*. The *Leibgarden* consisted of the Halberdiers, Garde Carabiniers and Garde Grenadiers. All were mounted. The Halberdiers seem to have been ceremonial in function and wore blue with silver lace with a surtout of red edged in silver over the top. The Garde Carabinier and Garde Grenadiers had the same coat but with a blue surtout edged in silver. The schabraque for all three was blue edged silver and they had black horses. The Garde Grenadiers wore fur grenadier hats with a blue bag. The Carabinier and Grenadiers were formed in 1696. In 1701 and 1702 respectively they became the *Leibgarde erflart*.

In 1702 and 1705 two further regiments were added to the cuirassier. The second of these was one of carabiniers, modelled on the French style and recruited from the remains of the three dragoon regiments. Full details of the cuirassier uniforms are shown in the uniform chart, however a few additional points can be made. They appear to have continued to use the lobster tail helmet while also being issued with the tricorn. The cuirass was blackened. Trumpeters wore coats in the regimental colours with false sleeves and white lace including chevrons up each arm. Officers also wore coats of the regimental colours with the blue and silver sash. All schabraques, as well as having lace around the edge, had a diagonal lace of the same colour cutting off the rear corner. The Carabinier was the only non-cuirassier regiment in the Bavarian horse.

Dragoons. In 1700 there were three regiments of dragoons. These were Schier that became Santini in 1701, Arco that became Fels in 1699 and then became Torring - Seefel in 1703, and Monasteroi. The style of dress had changed little from the latter years of the previous century. Like other dragoons they were dressed in much the same way as the horse but with hats and no cuirass. In 1704, after Blenheim, the three dragoon regiments were disbanded and the remains formed into the Prince Philip Carabineers. No further dragoon regiments were formed in the Bavarian army during the war.

Hussars. From about 1704 to 1706 Bavaria had a hussar regiment Locatelli. Blue dolmans with white loops were worn with white pear shaped buttons, blue breeches and silver and white worsted sashes. Hats of fox fur with blue bags were also worn and blue sabretaches with white embroidery. The schabraque was blue edged white.

Artillery. In 1701 the artillery wore grey coats with blue cuffs and lining. The waistcoat was also blue. The hat was a black tricorn.

Illustrations

A Carabineer	B Liebregiment 1700	C Grenadier 1704
D Dragoon 1700	E Cuirassier	F Hussar
G Artillery 1700		

BAVARIAN HORSE AND DRAGOONS

REGIMENT

	Coat	Lining	Cuffs	W/coat	Breeches	Schabraque	Remarks
HORSE							
Arco previously Haraucourt	Iron Grey	Blue	Blue	Blue	Blue or Leather	Sky blue edged white.	White cravat
Latour became Costa	Iron Grey	Green	Green	Grey	Grey		
SalburgWeidel also Roth	Iron Grey	Deep Rose Red	Deep Rose Red	Grey or Leather	Grey or Leather	Deep Rose Red edged white	Yellow buttons
Wolframsdorff Locatelli	Iron Grey	Sky Blue	Sky Blue	Sky Blue	Leather	White with sky blue edge	White buttons, black cravat
Prince Philip's Carabinier	Sky Blue	Scarlet	Scarlet	Leather	Sky Blue	Scarlet with silver edge.	Coat of arms Gilt buttons and gold shoulder knot. Black tricorn edged silver
DRAGOONS							
Arco	Red	Blue	Blue	Blue		Blue edged white	Blue cloak
Monaseroi	Red	Yellow	Yellow	Yellow		Yellow edged white	Another source gives blue faced grey
Sohier became Santim	Red	Red	Red	Green		Green edged white	Red Cloak

BAVARIAN FOOT

REGIMENT

	Coat	Lining	Cuffs	W/coat	Breeches	Stockings	Remarks
Leibregiment							
Fusiliers	Sky Blue	Blue	White	Sky Blue	Sky Blue	Grey	Black tricorn edged silver.
Grenadiers	Sky Blue	Sky Blue	Sky Blue	Sky Blue	Sky Blue	Grey	Coat had 20 wide and 13 narrow silver bars. 1704 black conical bearskin, red bag silver lace and tassel.
Kurprince or Prince Electoral	Sky Blue	Sky Blue	Sky Blue	Sky Blue	Sky Blue	Grey/White	Four wide and 8 narrow white loops on coat. Silver lace on hat. Grenadiers hat brown fur, red bag, white lace
Mercy previously Haxthausen	Sky Blue	Red	Red	Sky Blue	Sky Blue	Grey/White	Black hat laced white.NCOs had red coats with sky blue cuff etc.
Maffei	Sky Blue	Yellow	Yellow	Sky Blue	Sky Blue	Grey	Black hat laced white with blue and white cockade. Tin buttons
Lutzenberg	Sky Blue	Red	Red	Red	Red	Grey	Black hat laced white with blue and white cockade. Tin buttons
Tattenback previously Rivera	Sky Blue	Bright Yellow	Bright Yellow	Bright Yellow	Sky Blue	Red or Grey	Black hat laced white with blue and white cockade. Tin buttons
Spilberg	Sky Blue	Red, later Dark Blue	Red, later Dark Blue	Dark Grey	Dark Grey	Grey	Black hat laced white
d'Octfort	Sky Blue	Sky Blue	Sky Blue	Grey	Sky Blue	Grey	
Bettendorf	Sky Blue	Red	Red	Red	Pale Blue	Pale Blue	Tin buttons

THE BRITISH ARMY

Marlborough's campaigns in the War of the Spanish Succession (1702-12) provide British history with some of its most famous and successful battles. The British army with which Marlborough achieved these successes with was still recovering from a less than successful campaign in the Low Countries 10 years before. It was however the product of the military turbulence of the late 17th century and already had much of the character and experience that would provide firm foundations to build on throughout the century and into the Napoleonic Wars.

Regiments of this time were usually raised and commanded by their colonels. There were very few major changes in the period 1700-20, from that of the preceding decade, but rather a continuing and gradual evolution that made a visible difference to the appearance of the troops that fought in these battles.

THE CHANGING SIZE OF THE ARMY

Under William III the army had experienced rapid growth to cope with the various conflicts. When the war in Europe came to an end with the Treaty of Ryswick in 1697 there was no need to maintain such a large standing army. As is often the case the process of reducing the army was speedy and excessive. When the war in Europe again became imminent at the turn of the century and England was required, under its 1668 treaty obligations, to provide military assistance to Holland, new troops had to be found.

A

B

In 1701 there were 12 battalions to be found from Ireland for the Low Countries and a further four for the West Indies. So within 15 months of the massive disbandment, the Irish garrison was depleted by 15 out of its 21 battalions. Four new battalions were raised immediately. Further demands for troops in Holland caused a further 15 new regiments to be raised in 1702. In addition to the foot, six regiments of marines were raised including one old regiment. In 1703 another five new battalions were raised, named after their colonels. In the same year there was a requirement to send troops to the Iberian Peninsula. These came from Flanders and resulted in a new regiment of dragoons being raised for Flanders and a further seven regiments of foot of which four were raised in Ireland. In 1706 a further regiment of dragoons and 11 regiments of foot were formed in the spring and a twelfth regiment was added later in the year. In the same year Barrymore's Foot, in Spain, became Pearce's Dragoons although some of the officers went home to raise another battalion and thus Barrymore's Foot continued to exist. In 1707 a further five battalions of foot were raised. In 1710 further regiments were raised, five of these being Huguenot dragoon regiments and two further regiments of foot.

Even before the Peace of Utrecht was concluded, the process of disbanding the army had begun again. In 1712 a total of 13 regiments of dragoons and 22 of foot were disbanded. More disbandment followed when the treaty was concluded. Behind these disbandments was a political motivation, inspired by Bolingbroke and Ormonde, to eliminate those officers and units who had favoured the Protestant succession. This pro-Jacobite influence resulted in many of the more senior and established regiments being listed for disbandment. This included not only the forbears of the 7th and 8th Dragoons, but also those of the 6th, 14th, 22nd, 28th, 29th, 30th, 32nd, 33rd and 34th Foot.

The death of Queen Anne in 1714, the succession of George I, Elector of Hanover, and the return of Marlborough to royal favour put an end to the disbandments but not before the army had again been greatly reduced.

THE INFANTRY

Headdress. The black broad brimmed felt hat, first with one side turned up, then two, had by the turn of the century developed into the more familiar tricorn hat with the edge bound in yellow or white lace. The grenadier hat in this period continued to vary from regiment to regiment. The Foot Guards and the 18th Royal Irish had the stiffened bag, wearing the hat high in the mitre style. Others let the bag drop down to side or rear whilst yet another style had a fur band. The non-fur cap usually had a tassel on the end of the bag and a grenade and cypher or badge on the front.

Coat. The single breasted coat of the late 1680s had changed little in style by the turn of the century. The collar was not yet in general use although the 1st Foot Guards had them. The coat was often worn with the upper half open, showing the waistcoat and perhaps the lining in a way that would later lead to the introduction of lapels. The bottom of the skirt was not yet turned back, as was later to be the fashion. Most regiments now had their grenadier company's coats decorated with braid across the chest, on the buttonholes, cuffs and pockets. Cuffs were generally lower down the arm showing less of the shirtsleeve than in the previous decade.

Waistcoat. Reports from 1708 show that in his 2nd year a soldier received "a good cloth coat lined as first year, waistcoat made of former year's coat." It would seem that the waistcoat would therefore be of the coat colour, the cuffs having presumably been cut off. It is however possible that the coat was turned inside out thus producing waistcoats of the lining colour.

Greatcoats and Surtouts. Greatcoats or surtouts were issued as an essential part of campaign dress.

Breeches. A pair of "good kersey breeches" was issued. There were now close fitting and less like the pantaloons of the previous decade, thus dispensing with the need for coloured ties or garters.

Shirts. Two good shirts and a neck cloth were issued.

Stockings. Stockings were issued and worn on campaign.

Gaiters. The gaiters were probably introduced piecemeal in response to the appalling weather conditions when campaigning in Flanders. It seems likely that there were a variety of colours and materials. It is recorded that in 1703 the 4th Foot were issued with buff gaiters.

D

Shoes. Buckled shoes, though still high tongued, were issued replacing those tied with bows.

Knapsacks and Waterbottles. Knapsacks were worn over the shoulder and a variety of non-issued water bottles were worn. In addition a proportion would carry kettles or cooking pots.

EQUIPMENT

Musketeers. The musketeers' equipment progressed with the transition from matchlock to flintlock musket. By this period the bandolier had fully disappeared. The cartridge pouch was worn on the right hip supported from a broad shoulder belt. The waist belt supported the short sword or hanger on the left hip and also the bayonet. The latter was either the old plug bayonet or increasingly the more efficient socket bayonet, which was replacing the former.

Pikemen. The pikemen had almost disappeared from the army by the start of the period with the pikes finally being withdrawn in 1702. The half pike remained as a weapon and badge of rank.

Grenadiers. The grenadier company was now a standard part of the English regiment during this period. They were used increasingly as elite troops rather than as grenadiers. In 1705 hand grenades ceased to be issued for the 4th Foot and that they wore a pouch belt as for musketeers. This may not have been typical for the 4th Foot were on marine service at the time. It does seem likely that this gradually happened to the infantry in general.

Musicians. The drummers and hautbois players were on a regiment's establishment by this stage with two drummers per company. Uniforms in reverse colours were now the norm and dress otherwise had changed little except the hat, in common with the musketeers, was tricorn style.

Officers. Apart from uniforms of a finer quality and considerable lace of silver or gold which marked officers but not rank, officers carried a half pike or espontoon. Crimson waist sashes were now usual.

Sergeants. The sergeants wore uniforms of similar pattern but better quality than the soldiers. They frequently had lace or silver or gold. They carried a halberd as a badge of rank.

THE CAVALRY

Headwear. By this time the headwear was the tricorn probably with the metal cap or 'pot' inside. There is some evidence that the black cockade also made its appearance as early as 1704, although this precedes the more frequently expressed view that it was the black cockade of Hanover formally introduced in 1715. Dragoons generally wore the tricorn as well although horse grenadiers and at least the Scots Greys wore grenadier style caps.

Coat. The coat was single breasted following the body down to the waist with a full skirt finishing at or just above the knee. It had large full cuffs and large buttoned

G

pockets. It was worn open (showing the cuirass underneath in the case of the horse). The button holes and buttons were frequently decorated with tape across the chest, on the pockets, cuffs and seams. The coat was without collar although the Royal Dragoons fitted blue collars in Spain.

Waistcoat. The waistcoat (worn under the cuirass for the horse) was frequently of the regimental facing colour. They were made of cloth though some regiments may have reverted to leather or buff for better protection during the war.

Greatcoats. From about 1685 a form of overcoat began to be issued to the infantry. They were an important element of campaign dress alleviating some of the hardship caused by the weather.

Breeches. Breeches were often of the regimental colour. They were made of shag, that is worsted cloth with a velvet nap on one side.

Shirts and Cravats. Shirts began to be issues at the turn of the century and were usually worn with a cravat.

Stockings. These, although not visible when worn with boots, were issues and usually white.

Boots. The boots worn by both the horse and dragons were black high jackboots. Although the style was the same it may well be that those of the dragoons were softer and more supple to allow for dismounted action.

Cloak. Issued with lining of regimental colour and carried as a roll on the back of the saddle.

Gloves. Gloves were issued to dragoons.

Belts. The characteristic cross belts for sword and carbine continued for horse but dragoons now had a waist belt for the sword while the belt over the left shoulder supported the cartridge pouch.

H

Horse Equipment. Saddles was heavier than nowadays. The seat was cloth, plush or velvet and the "skirts" were leather with ornamental stitching. Stirrups were normal. The schabraque or saddlecloth was square in appearance with slightly rounded corners. It was usually of the regimental colour or scarlet with a border lace or tape trim. The holster caps were of the same colour as the saddlecloth with a trim. Frequently they were ornamented with a crown and cypher or other badge. The pistol holsters were leather tipped with metal.

Arms. A pair of pistols was carried by all cavalry, but in 1697 these were discontinued for the dragoons. The horse regiments carried the carbine, a short firelock with a smaller bore than the fuzil. The snaphance musket was issued to dragoons in 1687. They also carried bayonets. Swords were non-standard but generally heavy straight bladed with a three-bar hilt and black leather scabbard.

EQUIPMENT

Horse. At the start of this period the regiments of horse were equipped much as the dragoons, the cuirass having been taken out of service in 1698. However the front plate only was re-issued out of store in 1707 and remained in service until 1714 when it went back to store. The cuirass was underneath the coat and over the waistcoat, the coat generally being worn open. This small change however produced a distinct difference between the look of the horse. The characteristic cross belts and similar weapons of the previous period were retained.

Dragoons. Unlike the previous decade, the dragoons were used more as cavalry than mounted infantry. The tricorn was replacing the grenadier type cap. In 1699 the equipment consisted of a carbine belt and a waist belt with cartouche box, sword and bayonet. The waist belt therefore distinguished the dragoons who now had only one shoulder belt for carbine.

Horse Grenadiers. Some regiments, in addition to the Life Guards, raised horse grenadiers. Among these were certainly the 2nd Dragoons or Scots Greys and the 5th Dragoons. They were equipped and dressed as grenadiers but with cavalry boots.

Musicians. The presence of military musicians continued. Each dragoon troop had a drummer and hautbois player, the latter being later increased to two. The regiments of horse had a kettledrummer and two trumpeters. The dragoons had side drummers although as early as 1700 there is evidence of a kettledrummer but not on the establishment.

Officers. Officers continued to have uniforms of better material with silver or gold lace. The waistcoat, often buff, was also laced in silver or gold. Swords were worn on waist belts under coats and usually with a waist sash. The saddlecloth and housings were also heavily laced and embroidered.

Sergeants. The sergeants were generally dressed as the troopers but with better quality cloth and again, although less elaborately, with silver or gold lace.

Horses. The custom of black horses for both regiments of horse and dragoons was now dominant although there were exceptions such as the 3rd Regiment of Horse (later 2nd Dragoon Guards (The Queen's Bays)) and the Royal North British Dragoons (later the Royal Scots Greys). At this time too, Cadogan, the Quartermaster General, introduced the habit of docking the horses' tails down to just a few inches.

THE ARTILLERY

It seems likely that the artillery continued to wear red with blue cuffs and breeches until 1716 when the first two permanent companies of artillery were formed at Woolwich. These were dressed in blue coats with red cuffs, buff breeches and white stockings. They probably were both tricorn and had an undress cap of blue with a red bag. For Marlborough's train in 1703 the "Entry Book of Bills" reads:

Large Surtout Coat of crimson cloth, lined with blue shalloon & brass buttons, with pockets, for Sergeants, Corporals, Gunners and Pontoon Men 96 (sets).
Large Surtout Coats of red cloth, lined with blue shalloon, with brass buttons and pockets, for Matrosses and Pioneers   70 (sets).

MARINES

In 1702 orders were given for the raising of six marine regiments (Saundersons, Villiers, Fox's, Mordaunts, Holts and Shannon's, the last three being disbanded in 1713). Six other regiments, already in existence were to be for "sea service," that is "land forces to make descents or otherwise as occasion requires." These were the 6th, 19th, 20th, 34th, 35th, and 30th Foot. In addition the 4th Foot were made marines in 1703 and converted back to line regiment in 1711.

Marine uniforms were much the same as for the foot but with "high crowned leather caps covered with cloth of the regimental facing colour and ornamented with devices the same as the caps worn by the grenadiers." The sword may have been some form of cutlass. A pouch and bayonet were worn on the waist belt.

GENERAL STAFF

Information on the uniforms of the general staff is scarce in this period and what was worn seems largely optional. Much of what is known comes from the Blenheim tapestries. Coats are scarlet or blue with red cuffs, single breasted worn open with gold lace on the seams, down the front and on the buttonholes. The cuirass worn beneath the coat may well have been ornamental. Breeches were buff or scarlet. Sashes were worn across the shoulder or around the waist. The tricorn hat was bound in gold. The commander would carry a baton. Horse furniture was red with elaborate gold trim and embroidery.

In the tapestries are the runners, used for transporting less important messages. These were black peaked caps, coats of blue and white livery and a staff as a symbol of their authority.

Illustrations

A	Officer of Foot 1702
B	Ensign 1700s
C	Sergeant of Foot 1705, aftr a figure in the Marlburian tapestries at Blenheim
D	Grenadier 1705
E	Foot on the march 1705, after a figure in the Marlburian tapestries at Blenheim
F	Officer of Horses 1705
G	Dragoon 1702
H	Horse 1711
I	Artillery 1700
J	Dragoon 1702
K	Grenadier, 1st Foot Guards
L	Drummer 1705

BRITISH HORSE AND DRAGOONS

REGIMENT

	Coat	Facing	W/coat	Saddle	Remarks
REGIMENTS OF HORSE					
Life Guards	Scarlet	Troop Colour	Buff	Troop Colour	
Blues	Blue	Scarlet		Blue	
Lumley's, later 1st KDG	Red	Yellow	Yellow	Yellow	White lace on buttons?
Harvey's, later 2nd DG	Red	Buff			White loops on buttons down chest and pockets
Wood's, later 3rd DG	Red	Green	Green	Green Edged White	Leather breeches, white hat lace
Langston's, later 4th DG	Scarlet	White			
Cadogan's, later 5th DG	Red	Buff	Buff	Buff	1707 cuirass returns until 1714
	Red (1710)	Green	Green	Green	Green shag breeches replace buff or striped ones
Wyndham's Palmes's (from 1706), later 6th DG	Red	Sea Green	Sea Green	Sea Green	Silver lace on hat, cuffs and schabraque
Schomberg's.later 7th DG	Scarlet	Black? White?			
DRAGOONS					
Royal Regiment, later 1st Dragoons	Red	Blue			
Royal Scot's, Hay's Stairs from 1706, later 2nd Dragoons (Royal Scots Greys)	Red	Blue			
Lloyd's, Carpenters in 1703, later 3rd Dragoons then Hussars	Red	Blue?Red?	Blue	Blue	Yellow hat lace
Essex's later 4th Dragoons then Hussars	Red	Light Green	Light Green	Light Green	White hat lace
Royal Irish, Ross's later 5th Dragoons then 5th Lancers	Red				
Cunningham's, later 6th Inniskilling Dragoons	Scarlet				
Kerr's later 7th Dragoons then 7th Hussars	Red	White			
Conyngham's, Killigrew's from 1706, Peppers from 1707, later 8th Dragoons then 8th Hussars	Red	Yellow	Buff	Yellow	Edged White White tricorn lace and buttons
Pearce's	Red	Yellow			
Peterborough's, Nassau's from 1707, J. Stanhope's from 1710					
Guiseard's					
Rochford's, Lapell's from 1710					

BRITISH FOOT

REGIMENT

	Coat	Facing	W/coat	Breeches	Remarks
FOOT GUARDS					
1st Guards	Red	Royal blue	Red	Blue	Blue collar? Gold lace
Coldstream Guards	Red	Royal blue			
Scots Guards	Red	White, 1707 blue	White?		
FOOT					
Royal Regt. Orkney's (2 battalions) later 1st Foot Royal Scots.	Red	White then blue		Grey	Yellow hat lace
Queen Dowager's Bellasis's Portmore's in 1703, Kirkes in 1710. Became 2nd Foot.	Red	Sea green			
Buffs; C. Churchill's Argyll's from 1707, Selwyn's from 1711. Became 3rd Foot	Red	Buff	Buff called ash	Buff	White buttons and lace, white hat lace
Seymour's Marines 4th Foot	Red	Yellow	Red	Grey?	1703 buff gaiters. Marines 1704-10 Marine hat
Pearce's became 5th Foot	Red	Yellow Green		Green	
Rivers's, Southwell's from 1706, Harrisons from 1708 - became 6th Foot	Red	Yellow			
Royal Fusiliers, Tyrawley's became 7th Foot	Red	Blue From 1702			
Queen's, Webb's became 8th Foot	Red	Yellow			
Wm. Stewart's became 9th Foot	Red	Blue			
North & Grey's later 10th Foot	Red	Red			
Stanhope's, Hill's from 1705 later	Red	Yellow	Yellow 1705-6	Yellow 1705-6	
Livesay's later 12th Foot	Red	White		Blue	
Barrymore's (became Pearce's Dragoons 1706 but Barrymore's raised in 1708, later 13th Foot)	Red	Yellow	White 1706	White 1706	1702 yellow collar edged white. White lace on buttons and tricorn
John Tidcomb's Later 14th Foot	Red	Yellow			
Howes, Somerset's from 1709 - later 15th Foot	Red	Red			
Derby's, Godfrey's from 1705 - later 16th Foot	Red	White		White	
Bridge's, Blood's from 1703, Wightman's from 1707 -later 17th Foot		Grey?			
Royal Irish, Hamilton's Ingoldsby's from 1705 later 18th Foot	Red	Blue		White	
Erle's - later 19th Foot	Red	Yellow	?	Yellow	Brown gaiters. Tricorn edged white
G. Hamilton's, Newton's from 1706 - later 20th Foot	Red	White			
Scots Fusiliers, Row's Mordaunt's from 1704, De Lalo's from 1706, Mordaunt's from 1709, Orrery's from 1709-later 2lst Foot	Red	Red, Blue from 1712		Grey	Yellow stockings
T. Handasyd later 22nd Foot	Red	Buff			
Ingoldsby's, Sabine's from 1705 - later 23rd Foot	Blue	White		White Until 1714	
Seymour's, Marlborough's from 1702, Tattons from 1704, Primrose's from 1708 - later 24th Foot	Red	Green?			
The Edinburgh Regt. of Foot, Leven's, later 25th Foot	Red	Deep Yellow			
Cameronians, Ferguson's, Borthwick's from 1705. Stairs in 1706, Preston's from 1706 later 26th Foot	Red	White/Yellow?	White	White	Yellow tricorn lace, Grenadier hat white front and surround, red bag.
Inniskillings, Whethams later 27th Foot	Red	Blue			
Gibson's, De Lalo's from 1704, Mordaunt's from 1706, Windsor's from 1709 - later 28th Foot	Red	Yellow			
Farrington's - later 29th Foot	Red	Yellow		Blue	White stockings
Saunderson's Marines Pownall's from 1704 Will's from 1705 - later 30th Foot	Red	Yellow			
Villiers's Marines, Luttrell's from 1703 Churchill's from 1706, Goring's from 1711 - later 31st Foot	Red	Yellow			
Fox's Marines Borr's from 1704 later 32nd Foot	Red	Green			White lace
Huntingdon's, Leigh's from 1703, Duncanson's from 1705, Wade's from 1705 - later 33rd Foot	Red	Yellow		Yellow	White stockings

REGIMENT

REGIMENT	Coat	Facing	W/coat	Breeches	Remarks
Lucas's, H. Hamilton's later 34th Foot	Red	Light Grey or White	Grey	Grey	Yellow belt with "L" and crown. Officer - lace on jacket cuffs, pockets and hat silver.
Donegal's, Gorges's from 1706, later 35th Foot	Red	Orange			
Charlemont's, Almutt's from 1706, Argyll's from 1709, Disney's from 1710 - later 36th Foot	Red	Green			
Meredirh's, Windress's from 1710 - later 37th Foot.	Red	Yellow?			
Conte's, Sankey's from 1703 - later 39th Foot	Red				
Luke Lillingstone's later the 38th Foot	Grey? Red	Yellow			

REGIMENTS WHICH LATER DISBANDED

REGIMENT	Coat	Facing	W/coat	Breeches	Remarks
Stringer's, Argyll's from 1706, Orrery's from 1707, Sibourg's from 1710					
Temple's, Newton's from 1710					
Evan's, Macartney's, Sutton's from 1709					
Prendergast's, Macartney's from 1709, Kane's from 1711	Red	Green		Scarlet	1711 Sgt had silver lace on pocket sleeves and belt.
Wynne's	Red	Yellow	Yellow	Blue	1705 - yellow and blue loops, 1708 grenadier cap red cloth. Sand yellow with wolves head embroidered on it. Loops were blue and white.
Townshend's, Honeywood's from 1709					
Brudenell's, Johnson's from 1708,					
C. Churchill's from 1709					
Mount joy's					
Gorges's, Allen's 1706, Moore's from 1707 and Molesworths from 1710					
J. Caulfield's, Bowles's from 1705					
Elliot's					
Mohun's, Dormers from 1708					
T. Caulfield's, Creighton's from 1708					
Breton's, Buttler's from 1711				Willow green	
Stanwix's	Red	Yellow			Brass buttons
Dungannon's, Monrandre's from 1706					
Watkin's, Rich's 1709					
Hotham's,					
Mark Kerr's					
Paston's, Frank's 1710					
Inchiquin's, Stanhope's from 1710, Nassau's from 1711	Red				Officers coat scarlet
Lepell's, Richard's from 1710 and Stanhope's from 1711					
Munden's					
Gore's					
Rooke's					
Price's					
Fielding's					
E. Jones's					
Slanes'					
Tyrell's					

THE DANISH ARMY

INTRODUCTION

Between 1685 and 1720 the Danish army was involved almost continuously in war between east and west Europe. The wars in the east are not the concern of this book, but one must not forget that the Danish also played a part, as an ally of Saxony and Poland, in the Great Northern War. In the west Denmark was also committed on the side of the allies due to her close ties with the Dutch and the army of William III. In addition some Danish units were in the service of the Austrian Emperor.

After a short break between 1697 and 1701 following the war of the League of Augsburg (1689-1697) Denmark's forces were once again involved in war in western Europe. At the outset of the War of the Spanish Succession, Denmark refused France's offer of alliance and instead made her army available to the allies. Denmark hired out forces to both the Austrian Empire and the allies (England, Holland and the German States), in the Low Countries. Approximately 8,000 men went to the Emperor. These fought in northern Italy fighting at Mantua and Luzarra and were later used to quell revolt in Hungary. They returned to Denmark, a much depleted force, in 1709. The Danish Corps in the Low Countries referred to as being "in the service of the Maritime Powers" started in 1701 at 1200 strong. From then on they fought at many of the major battles including Blenheim, Oudenarde and Malplaquet gaining a considerable reputation. They finally returned to Denmark in 1713 and 1714. By then they had been reinforced and expanded several times. At its height the Corps consisted of eight regiments of horse, one of dragoons and seven infantry regiments.

THE UNIFORMS

The details of specific regimental uniforms are given on the separate table. The following paragraphs give general details of the dress.

The Foot. The uniform of Danish National Regiments was grey, usually with a regimental distinctive colour for the lining, cuffs and frequently the breeches and stockings. The coat was of similar in design to other European armies. The black hats were turned up, first on one side and by 1704 in tricorn style. The hat had a yellow or white braid on the edge and a rosette. The coat frequently had lace around the buttonholes. The equipment was of natural leather colour and consisted of a waist belt worn over the coat for both sword and bayonet. A black cartridge pouch hung from a shoulder belt of leather onto the right hip. Shoes were black with buckles. Drummers wore the same colour uniform as the soldiers.

A

B

C

The Horse. The Horse were dressed much as other European cavalry of the time. They wore a full-skirted coat, vest, skin or hide breeches and high boots. In 1701 the troopers were issued with black breastplates and cuirass. The officers' cuirass had the King's initials in brass under the front edge of the neck and had brass rivets round the edges. Cross straps supported the sword, carbine and cartridge box. The cuirass was presumably worn over the coat and lined with the regimental facing colour but this is not clear. Schabraque and pistol covers were the usual style. The headwear was a black tricorn edged in lace and with a metal skullcap. Officers wore the same colour uniform as the men, but with gold lace and a yellow and red waist sash. The trumpeters generally had more elaborate uniforms with vertical lace or hoops of lace around the sleeves.

The Dragoons. Like other European dragoons, those of Denmark were equipped much like the horse but without the cuirass and on smaller mounts. Instead of a carbine they carried a musket and bayonet. They wore a lighter boot than the horse. It is not clear whether or not they wore fur hats in the manner of other dragoons but at least some regiments wore the tricorn.

Artillery. The Danish artillery regiment wore a violet coat lined green.

Post Script. In 1711 the national coat colour changed from light grey to red, but it is not known if this reached the maritime corps before they returned home to Denmark at the end at the war.

Illustrations
A   Danish Liebgarde
B   Danish Grenadier Corps
C   Danish Foot 1711

DANISH HORSE AND DRAGOONS

REGIMENT

	Coat	Lining	Cuffs	W/coat	Breeches	Schabraque	Remarks
Livgarden til Hest	Yellow	Red					Alternatively coat could have been red with yellow lining
Livregiment Til Hest	Grey	Yellow	Red	Leather	Leather	Red edged yellow	Gold hat lace. Yellow buttons
No 1 Sjaelland Regiment	Light Grey	Carmine					
No 2 Sjaelland Rytter Regiment	Light Grey	Purple red	Purple red	Buff	Buff	Yellow with red edge	Yellow hat lace
No 3 Sjaelland Regiment	Light Grey	Light blue					
No 1 Jydske Regiment	Light Grey	Grass green					
No 2 Jydske Rytterregiment Vettewig Brockdorff)?	Light Grey	Dark Blue	Dark Blue	Leather	Leather	Dark Blue edged yellow	Yellow hat lace, white cravat. Grey cloak lined blue
No 3 Jydske Rytter Regiment	Grey	Brown					
No 4 Jydske Rytterregiement	Grey	Isabelle					
No 5 Jydske Rytteylregiment (Von Schmettau)	Grey	Yellow	Yellow	Buff	Buff	Yellow with red edge	Yellow hat lace
1st Fynske	Light Grey	Light Green					
2nd Fynske	Light Grey	Orange					
Bernstorffs Regiment	Light Grey	Red					
Kyrasserregiment (1709)	Light Grey		Blue				Black cuirass
Ahlefeldts Kyrasserregiment Raised 1701, 1705 Wurttemberg	Light Grey	Blue					

DRAGOONS

	Coat	Lining	Cuffs	W/coat	Breeches	Schabraque	Remarks
Livregiment Dragoons	Crimson	White	White			White, edge crimson	
Holstenske Dragoons	Red	Green	Green			Red, green edge	Yellow collar. Light blue trim on hat
Wurtemberg-Oels Dragoons Rodsteen/Trampe	White/Grey Yellow	Yellow Orange					

DANISH FOOT

REGIMENT

	Coat	Lining	Cuffs	W/coat	Breeches	Stockings	Remarks
Livgarde Til Fods	Straw yellow	Carmine Red	Carmine Red	Carmine Red	Carmine Red or Straw yellow	Carmine Red	White hat lace, carmine rosette. Carmine ladder of lace up front of coat
Dronningens	Red	Yellow		Grey	Grey	White	Tricorn trimmed Yellow with yellow rosette. Grenadier cap yellow front plate bordered white with red bag.
Prince George	Light grey	Orange	Orange	Orange	Orange	Orange	White hat lace, yellow rosette. White buttons and button hole lace.
Prince Karl	Light grey	Yellow	Yellow	Yellow	Grey	Yellow	Untrimmed tricorn yellow rosette. Buttons white, white loops. White cravat
Sjalland	Light grey	Dark Blue	Dark Blue	Dark Blue	Dark Blue	Hat trim and rosette yellow.	Buttons white, white loops.
Fyen or Fynske	Dark or iron grey	Green	Green	Green	Green	Green	Tricorn trimmed Yellow with green and white rosette. White buttons and loops.
Oldenborg	Light grey	Blue		Blue	Grey	White.	Tricorn trim and rosette red.
Jydland	White or Light grey	Red	Red	Red	Grey	Red	Tricorn trim and red and White. Rosette red or yellow. White buttons and loops.
Prince Christian	Light grey	Crimson		Crimson	Grey	Crimson	Tricorn trim and rosette crimson. White buttons and loops.
Schacks regiment	Light grey	Burnt yellow					
Marine regiment	Light grey	White		White	White	White	
Wurttemberg-oels	Light grey	Yellow		Yellow	Grey	Yellow	White buttons and loops. Untrimmed tricorn yellow rosette
Grenaderkorps	Red	Blue	Blue trimmed white	Blue	Blue	Blue	Cap - High fronted plate, surround white with blue bag with white lace. White buttons and loops.

THE DUTCH ARMY

INTRODUCTION

The army of Holland in this war was only a part, all be it a major one, of the armies of the United Provinces. These provinces, which adjoined the Spanish Netherlands, were Holland, Zeeland, Utrecht, Friesland, Groningen, Overijssel and Guelderland. Each province provided forces roughly relative to its size and economy. For simplicity they will be referred to as the combined forces as the Dutch army.

BACKGROUND

Through the 1650s to the 1670s there had been three Anglo-Dutch wars. These were generally naval affairs. From 1688 onwards, the United Provinces were to be a major ally of England, not surprisingly with a shared monarch, William III, for part of the time. In the two major conflicts between 1690 and 1712 the two sides were to fight side by side.

Despite the presence of Marlborough as Commander in Chief and a considerable percentage of Britain's army in the Low Countries, the Dutch provided a major part of the coalition army in Flanders considerably outnumbering the English. This army had the well-tried infantry of the previous war (War of the League of Augsburg) as well as the rather more dubious horse. One innovation credited to the Dutch foot was the system, described elsewhere, of firing not by rank but by a series of firings. This system, adopted by the English, gave the Dutch a considerable advantage in firepower and control of musketry fire over the French. One may also suppose that under Marlborough's eye the Dutch horse were schooled in the English way, relying not on firepower but on shock action. As a generalisation it would be true to say that the result of a common sovereign until 1702, common experiences in several wars and the benefit of the same Captain General in the current war, the armies of Britain and Holland could work and fight on a common basis of understanding. The Dutch were also organised on quite similar lines to the English.

A

B

THE UNIFORMS

The Dutch followed the same lines in fashion and equipment as other armies of the period. The uniform chart gives examples of Dutch cavalry and infantry of the period. The following notes are designed to highlight the main features.

The Foot. The Dutch foot included Scots, Swiss and Walloon regiments. These were usually dressed in red in the case of the first two and green in the latter case. The remainder of the Dutch infantry, except the guard, generally dressed in grey by 1700. The coat was single breasted, tailored at the waist with a full skirt down to the knee. The cuffs were large and full and the jacket had no collar. Beneath the coat was a long waistcoat, white shirt, full breeches and stockings. Buckled shoes were worn. The tricorn of felt tended to be low

English - Dragoon, Conyngham's, Killigrew's from 1706, Peppers from 1707

© Bob Marrion 2004

41

English - Royal Regt. Orkney's (later 1st Foot Royal Scots).
The regiment originally had white cuffs but changed to blue perhaps in the late 17th
century although some sources show them white in this period).

© Bob Marrion 2004

Danish - Sjarland Ritter Regiment No 2

© Bob Marrion 2004

Danish - Infantry, Prince George Regiment Dutch

© Bob Marrion 2004

crowned. Grenadier hats had a high metal front with a crown of facing colour, with a pompom. At the back of the hat the bottom turned up and out. Drummers frequently wore reverse coat and lining colours. The infantry equipment consisted of brown leather waist belt for sword and bayonet and a broad shoulder belt of similar colour with a black cartridge belt. Officers wore a broad orange sash over the right shoulder hanging in a knot on or below the left hip. Their coats, cuffs, pockets and hats were laced with gold or silver. Gorgets were worn about the throat as an indication of rank.

The Horse. By 1700 almost all the Dutch horse were wearing coats of grey, all be they of different shades from pearl grey to iron grey. The coats had broad deep cuffs of the lining colour. Beneath the coat was a waistcoat either of leather or the facing colour. Stiff breeches and high boots completed the dress. They wore tricorn hats, presumably with a metal cap to protect the crown. The sword was suspended from a belt over the right shoulder. A pair of pistols was fitted under the pistol caps at the front of the saddle. It would appear that by and large the cuirass was not worn except by officers of some regiments and by specific cuirassier regiments. When in use it was worn over the jacket. It is difficult to generalise about the dress of the musicians except that red coats with false sleeves were frequently worn and heavy vertical lace was common. Like the foot, the officers wore an orange shoulder sash. Their coats, schabraques and hats were laced in silver or gold with plumes in the hat.

C

The Dragoons. Dragoons appear to be much less common in the Dutch army than one might expect for the time. They generally wore red rather than grey. This apart they appear to have been dressed and equipped much as the horse including the wearing of high boots. Some regiments had fur dragoon hats with bag while others wore the usual broad brimmed cavalry hat. Lace was worn on the buttonholes and pockets.

The Artillery. There is little evidence of the uniforms of the Dutch artillery of this period. From a Knotel illustration, the dress in 1680 was blue coat with red cuffs and blue breeches, and for officers, red stockings.

Illustrations
A   Dutch Foot 1700
B   Dutch Guard 1705
C   Dutch Horse 1690

DUTCH HORSE AND DRAGOONS

REGIMENT

	Coat	Lining	Cuffs	W/coat	Breeches	Schabraque	Remarks
No 2 Horse Guards	Blue	Red				Red	
No 3 Nassau-Sarrebruck Eck	1689 Red 1703 Light Grey	Red Green	Red Green	- Green		- Green	Officer may have worn green coats with crimson cuffs.
No 4 Montpouillan, Maduran	Grey/white	Grey/White	Grey/white				
No5 Waldeck, Sachsen-Heilburg	White	Rose red	Rose red	Leather	Leather	Rose red edged white	White hat lace
No 6 Lintelo, Ruysch, Warfuse, van Eck	White	Red	Red	Red			
No 7 d'obdam, Dockum, d'issum, Pallandt	Grey	Red					
No 8 Flodroff, Rhoo, Drimborn	Grey/white	Red					
No 11 Berlo, Steyn, Hoornberg	Cinder grey	Red	Red	Red	Red	Red edged white	Officers coat red. Black tricorn edged white.
No 14 Van Oyen, Rechteren, Hoornberg	Dark grey	Dull Red	Dull Red				
No ? Athlone, Cannenberg, Diesbergen Reinhard	Grey	Scarlet	Scarlet	Scarlet	Leather	Scarlet edged white	White hat lace
ZEALAND							
No 19 Gardes Du Corps	Dark Crimson	Blue	Blue	Chamois Yellow		Dark Blue	White Horses
No 20 Weybnom, Huybert, Rammingen, Noorddeuringen	1695 White	Red	Red				
No 3, (Wurtembergers)	White	Black	Black	Leather	Leather	Black edged white	White hat lace
GUELDRE							
No 1 Willem, Nieuwenhuys, van Reede, Vincent	1690 Grey		Blue		Red		
No 21 Van Reeck, van Isendoorn, van Nijvenheim, Reinhard	Buff Yellow		Scarlet	Scarlet		Scarlet	
Aughrim, Athlone	White	Light Blue	Light Blue	Buff	Buff	Red edged yellow	Yellow hat rim. Copper buttons.
FRISE							
Gardes Du Corps Du Stadholder of Frise	1720 Blue, blue collar	Blue	Blue	Yellow			Gold buttons, lace on chest and cuffs
Nassau Friesland	Medium Blue	Red	Red	Leather or Red	Leather	Red edged white.	Black hat edged silver
GRONINGEN							
No27 Hessen-Homburg	Silver Grey	Silver Grey	Silver Grey				White buttons
DRAGOONS							
No 1 Coerland, Garde Dragoons (1678) William III, Hesse Cassel	Grey						Brown fur bonnet with red badge
No 2 Groben, Marwitz, Schlippenback	Grey	Blue	Blue				Officer's coat dark blue with blue cuffs
No 3 Dopff	Grey	White	White	White	White	White edged Red	White hat trim

DUTCH FOOT

REGIMENT	Coat	Lining	Cuffs	W/coat	Breeches	Stockings	Remarks
HOLLAND							
No 4 Dutch Guard	Indigo Blue	Red	Red	Blue	White	White	Tricorn braided yellow with yellow buttons
No 6, Waldeck, Holstein-Ploon, Oudenstein	Pearl Grey	Red	Red				
No 6, Hornes, Kessel	Dark Blue	Red					
Touroud de Saint Amant	1698 Grey	Light Blue	Light Blue	Light Blue			
No 8, Birkenfeld, Huffel	White	Red					
No 11, Tassin de Torsay	1698 Red	Yellow					
No 13, Zobel, Goor, d'Yvoy	White	Red	Red				Yellow buttons
No 15, Fagel, Welderen	1690 Red 1704 Grey /White	Yellow Yellow				Red	
No 17, Slangenburg	1708 White	White	Carmine Red	Grey	Grey	Grey	White hat lace
No 51, Goes, Holstein-Beck	1690 Red	Blue	Blue				
GUELDRE							
No 1, Van Bulow	1690 Pearl Grey	Blue	Blue	Blue	Blue		Yellow buttons, black hat edged gold
Van Welderen	1703 Indigo Blue	Indigo Blue	Indigo Blue	Indigo Blue	Grey		
No 2 (Fusiliers) Van Wijnebergen, Van Beynheym, Van Deelen	Grey/White	Red	Grey/White Or Red	Grey/White	Grey	Grey	NCOs red w/coat and breeches. No lace on hat.
No 3, Van Essen, Van Plettenberg	Ash Grey	Yellow				White	White buttons
No 18 Brandenbourg Donhoff, Cronstrom, Holsten	Grey 1702 Indigo Blue	Blue Red	Blue Red	Blue Red	Blue Red	Blue	Red cravat and white lace on hat
No 19 Salm, Dohna-Ferassieres	Grey	Blue	Blue				
No 20 Walloon	White		Red				Officers in crimson or Red coat
No 21, Lannoy Schoonenburg, Holstein Norburg	White/Grey	Red	Red				Red cravat
No 22, Allebrandsweed Amelisweerd	1702 Peal Grey	Red		Red	Red		
No 27, Van Weede, Van Nassau	1703 Grey	Grey, Sgts crimson lining	Grey, Officers red	Officers and Sgts Red		Officers red, Sgts crimson	Officers Gold lace
No 28, Ram, Hertaing, Werner, Blanche, Van Lennep, Van Dorth	Grey	Yellow	Yellow	Yellow			Grenadier regiment until 1709
No 29, Van Brunswick Luniburg, Osnabruck, Van Tettau, Van Keppel	Red	Yellow		Red?			
No 49, Heeckeren, Van Els	Red	White	White				Yellow buttons
No 50 Friesheim	Grey	Blue	Blue	Blue	Blue	Blue	Black tricorn edged yellow. Blue grenadier hat, yellow front plate and curled up at back.
ZEALAND							
No 23, Nassau Sarrebruck, Beke	1703 Grey/white	Red	Red				Black tricorn, gold trim, yellow buttons.
No 30, Van Haersolte, Van Salm, Rauck	1690 Red	Black	Red				
No 31, Mirleau Dilliers, Solbert De Marsilly, Gerard, Van Waes, Hass, Tulleken	Pearl Grey	Red	Red	Grey	Grey	Grey	Yellow hat lace

FRISE

Regiment	Coat	Cuffs	Lapels	Col4	Col5	Col6	Notes
No 33, Nassau Friesland	Blue	Red	Red	Red	Red	Red	White lace on button holes and hat
No 36, Schel Tinga, Van Claerbergen	White	Red	Red				Sgts had red coats laced white, officers red coats laced gold
No 37, Stirum, Brockhcrst, Coghoorn, Idzinga	Grey/White	Blue	Blue				White buttons

OVERIJSSEL

Regiment	Coat	Cuffs	Lapels	Col4	Col5	Col6	Notes
No 39, Coeverden, Ootmarssum	White or Grey						Officers coats dark red

GRONINGEN

Regiment	Coat	Cuffs	Lapels	Col4	Col5	Col6	Notes
No 43, Nassau, Holtzappel, Wickers	Blue		Red	Chamois	Chamois	Red	
No 44, Gockinga, Prott Ripperda	White	White	White. Sgts crimson cuffs, Officers Red cuffs				Yellow buttons

SCOTS IN DUTCH SERVICE

Regiment	Coat	Cuffs	Lapels	Col4	Col5	Col6	Notes
Murray	Red	White	White	White	White	White	Black tricorn edged white, white buttons
Portmore, 1703 Dalrymple, 1706 Borthwick, 1706 Heyburn, 1709 Douglas.	Red	Yellow	Yellow	Yellow	Yellow	Yellow	Yellow buttons Fusilier cap with yellow front, red bag, 2 red doves on front, yellow tassel on bag.
Colyear	Red (Carmine)	White	White	White	White	Grey/white	White hat lace

SWISS IN DUTCH SERVICE

Regiment	Coat	Cuffs	Lapels	Col4	Col5	Col6	Notes
Albemarle	Indigo Blue	Red Carmine	Red Carmine				
Lochmann	Red Carmine	Light Gold	Light Gold	Light Gold	Light Gold	Carmine	
Schmid de Gruneck	Indigo Blue	Red Carmine	Red Carmine	Red Carmine	Red Carmine	Red Carmine	White hat lace
Sturler	Indigo Blue	Red	Red Carmine	Red Carmine	Red Carmine	Red Carmine	Yellow hat lace Carmine

THE FRENCH ARMY

INTRODUCTION

A

The French army of the start of this period was not the massive, well-practised military machine which some writers would have one believe. Between 1659 and 1672 the infantry for example had been more than halved leaving just 62 regiments. The same was equally true of the other arms. The gradual process of growth did not begin again until perhaps 1680. At this stage there were 70 infantry regiments and some garrison battalions. In 1684, 30 of the latter became line infantry regiments. For the war in the 1690s France could not use just the existing and seasoned troops but required to create new regiments. Disbandment took place between the wars but again many fresh regiments had to be raised to bring the French infantry up to the 280 regiments which existed at one stage in the War of the Spanish Succession. While France therefore had a much larger standing army than her enemies it was not possible to fight the coming war on what had previously existed.

At least part of the reason for supposing that the French army was on a better footing than others in Europe can be attributed to the work of Viscount de Turenne, an innovative commander, and the Marquis de Louvois, Minister of War. These two famous reformers undoubtedly played an important part in the evolution of France's army. Turenne only contributed significantly to that army or part of the army that he had commanded. Once he left, or units left his command they were no longer subject to his innovations. As a result while Turenne made large improvements of in his own command they cannot be seen as an army wide reform. Louvois brought the army very much under the King's direct control whereas previously regimental and other commanders had a great deal of independence. His reforms resulted in common uniforms, marching in step, uniform weapons, equipment and a sound system of basic administration but the task of organising such a large and diverse organisation was beyond one man.

For these reasons among others, the French army was as immature, if not more so, than many of its European neighbours.

THE ARMY IN GENERAL

The dress and equipment, uniform styles and fashion in this period were much the same as that of other armies. Uniforms were in their infancy and dress regulations did not exist until 1690 when they were produced for the cavalry. For the infantry, uniform information is even less precise. Each branch of the army will be covered in turn.

MAISON DU ROI

The Maison du Roi were the Royal Household troops of France. Some of the units dated from the 15th century. Some had full military functions, others ceremonial and household guards and some combined both roles.

Gardes Du Corps. There were four companies of Gardes du Corps armed and equipped as cavalry. They wore blue coats (turquoise) with red lining and possibly red cuffs and breeches. They were responsible for security within the Louvre. They wore elaborate silver lace and by the War of the Spanish Succession, a black tricorn trimmed silver. Each company had a shoulder belt of company distinguishing colour and silver, which supported the sword. This colour was probably also that used for the schabraque. The companies and their colours were as follows.

Premiere Compagnie Ecossaise - silver and white, check belt.
Premiere Compagnie Francaise - silver and green, check belt.
Second Compagnie Francaise - silver and blue, check belt.
Troisieme Compagnie Francaise - silver and yellow, check belt.

Compagnie des Gendarmes. One company armed and equipped as cavalry and dressed in red. It is known that by 1720 they had cuffs of black plush, a yellowish buff waistcoat, red breaches and schabraque. All were laced in gold, as was the black tricorn, which also had a white feather trim.

Compagnie des Chevau Legers. One company dressed in red much as the Gendarmes with black cuffs and gold lace. The schabraque was red edged in gold.

Les Mousquetaires. Two companies of musketeers. They both wore scarlet coats, facings, cuffs and breeches. Over the coat was a *soubreveste*, something like a loose fitting, sleeveless long coat in blue and belted round the waist. The *soubreveste* had a white cross on the front and back with red flames behind the cross. The headdress was black tricorn with appropriate lace edge and white feather trim. The schabraque and pistol covers were red edged with lace. The horse colour and the lace identified the two companies.

Premiere Compagnie (Mousquetaires Gris [grey]) - gold lace.
Seconde Compagnie (Mousquetaires Noir [black]) - silver lace.

They were armed, equipped and fought as cavalry.

Grenadiers a Cheval. One company formed in 1676 was the most recent addition to the Maison du Roi. They wore a blue coat with red cuffs, facings and waistcoat. The schabraque pistol covers and caps were blue with silver edging on all but the caps. The hat had a rigid red bag, crescent shaped and upright, edged in white lace. The whole had a brown fur surround. The musket hung from a shoulder belt of buff edged silver.

Gendarmes. The Gendarmerie, not to be confused with the company of Gendarmes already covered, originated from the men at arms (*gens d'armes*) of medieval times. They are mentioned briefly now in this section on the Maison du Roi although they were not really a part. They were however second only to the Maison du Roi and will be covered in the section on cavalry.

The infantry of the Maison du Roi were as follows:

Gardes Francaises. The Gardes Francaises originated in the middle of the 16th century. They had a varying number of battalions and at one stage in Louis XIV's time they numbered almost 10,000 strong. They were equipped as infantry. They were dressed in royal blue coats with cuffs, waistcoat, stockings and breeches of scarlet. White lace decorated the coat and waistcoat buttons, the pockets and cuffs. These were in groups of three[*] by 1697 and may have been so before, although some illustrations (c.1684)

D

show the jacket edged down the front rather than across the buttonholes. Epaulettes of red loops were worn on both shoulders but these had disappeared by 1700. The pikemen retained the back and breastplates until about the same time. Musketeers wore bandoliers and shoulder belts in 1685, but by 1697 they had been replaced with brown leather cartridge boxes worn on a shoulder belt and a waistbelt for the sword and bayonet. The hat was black, edged silver and turned up at each side but did not take on the tricorn appearance until 1700. In 1697 the hat had red plumes which hung from one corner.

Gardes Suisses. The Regiment de Gardes Suisses date from 1616. They too had a number of battalions and were established and equipped in a similar way to the Grades Francaise who took precedence ever them. The coat was red with blue cuffs, lining, waistcoat, breeches and stockings. Lace, like that of the Gardes Francaises, was silver and crossed the front of the coat, waistcoat and pockets also cuffs in groups of three. The hat was black edged white and by 1700 it had assumed the tricorn style. Pikemen and musketeers would be equipped as for the Gardes Francaises.

Briefly, other sections of the Maison du Roi, used for ceremonial and guard duties were as follows:

Gardes de la Porte. (Guards of the Door). They were 50 strong and their duty was to guard the interior of the palace during the day. They wore elaborate uniforms with blue coats, red waistcoats, cuffs, breeches and stockings. The lace, which covered the seams, cuffs and formed a lattice across the chest, was gold and silver.

Cent-Gardes Suisses. The Cent-Gardes Suisses were formed in 1496 although their origins were even earlier. They too were used to guard the doors, specifically those of royal rooms. Their military uniform was a blue coat red cuffs, waistcoat and breeches, stockings and gold lace. On palace duty they wore elaborate Swiss costumes and carried halberds. They went immediately before the King on processions.

Gardes de la Prevote. (Provost Guards). These, as the name implies, were provost staff connected with the law. They preceded the Cent-Gards Suisses in procession. They looked after the law and legal aspects about the sovereign. They wore very splendid tunics with elaborate tabards in silver, gold, red and blue.

Garde de la Marche. (Guards of the Sleeve). They were 25 strong and were selected from the Scottish company of the Gardes du Corps. They were ceremonial guards who stood either side of and protected the king. Six were specially selected from this guard and formed the Garde Ecossais for specific ceremonies. The Guards of the Sleeve wore white tabards embroidered in gold, red and blue coat of arms worn over a blue sleeved and red cuffed coat and red breeches and stockings. The Garde Ecossais wore a special all white uniform of satin with a white tabard heavily ornamented in gold. Both the Guards of the Sleeve and the Garde Ecossais carried halberds.

Summary. Having briefly covered all the representatives of the Maison du Roi at the time of Louis XIV it is the cavalry, often referred to as the "Maison du Roi," which formed an important part of the French Horse and the Gardes Francaises and Gardes Suisses, which formed the cream of the infantry at this time.

E

THE INFANTRY

The French line infantry were organised into regiments each of three battalions and each battalion was about 650 men strong.

The Equipment. French equipment went through a similar transition from pike to musket as occurred elsewhere although it seems that the France retained the pike for longer than their enemies across the channel. It was officially discontinued in 1699 but was probably not completely withdrawn until 1703. It was certainly still in use at the time of the Peace of Ryswich. The cartridge box was of large rectangular shape hung low on the right hip from a shoulder belt, and also had the powder flask and bayonet (or hatchet for grenadiers). The cover was reddish brown and bore the royal crest. The sword and bayonet were worn on a waist belt. The French were much slower to accept the flintlock than other countries, the weapon not being authorised until 1700. Previously captured flintlocks had been smashed up by order to prevent their use by their own men. Socket or ring bayonets replaced the plug bayonet in the 1690s, their invention in France being attributed to Marshal Vauban, the famous French engineer. Swords appear to have lacked any form of uniform pattern as with other armies, halberds, sometimes very elaborate, were the badge of rank for the sergeant.

F

The Dress. The first uniforms were not unlike civilian dress with a coat with large pockets, waistcoat, broad brimmed felt hats, baggy breeches or pantaloons, gaiters, stockings and shoes. Officers' clothing would be much finer in quantity but was frequently not uniform; matter which Louis XIV put right in the 1690s. These early uniforms for the French infantry generally consist of a light grey coat with regimental distinction being by colour of the waistcoat, breeches, cuffs and lining. Exceptions to the light grey were the King's regiments who wore blue coats and the Prince's regiments who wore red. Also the foreign regiments in French service had characteristic coat colours; for example the Irish and Swiss wore red and the German turquoise blue. The hat seems to have followed the same evolution as took place in England, first with one then two sides being turned up and by 1700 forming a crude tricorn.

Infantry Uniform. By about 1700 a degree of uniformity had established itself. Sadly there is no single document, nor for that matter comprehensive record of these early uniforms. Lienhart and Humbert (see Bibliography) give plates of the infantry dress before 1720. There has been considerable doubt cast on the reliability of this source. In the absence of other information however, these details, which are considerable, form the basis for the uniform table although other sources have also been used. It provides detail on virtually all the regiments that were involved in the War of the Spanish Succession and if this was the dress before 1720 one must assume that a good deal would be relative to the period 1701 to 1714. A major source of regimental

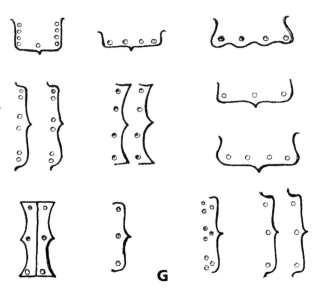

distinction was the number of buttons and pocket design. Pockets, which are illustrated elsewhere, were either horizontal (cross), vertical (upright) and single or double. Pockets described as *demi ecussion* were shaped like escutcheon or shields. By 1710 the cartridge box was no longer suspended from the shoulder but worn to the front centre or front right of the waistbelt and was rather smaller. While the hat was worn now with three sides turned up it was probably not until shortly before 1720 that it took the rather rigid shape of the tricorn as it became known. The epaulettes had disappeared as a regimental distinction and breeches were now tight fitting and no longer had elaborate garter bows which had been used with the baggier pantaloons previously. The stockings were worn above the knee.

Infantry Drummers. The infantry drummers generally wore *Petit livree de Roi*, a blue coat laced with white chains on a red background. They were a good many exceptions just a few of which were as follows.

Nettencourt - green coat
Lyonnais - green coat with orange and gold lace.
La Reine - red coat.
Bourbon - chamoise yellow
Dorington - orange coat.
O'Brien - yellow coat.
Aunis - red coat with grey cuff.
Des Landes - yellow coat.

The drum, suspended from a shoulder belt was often blue with the royal crest but again, as with the coat, there were many exceptions. Sometimes these exceptions followed the coat, for example, Lyonnais had a green drum. The breeches, waistcoat and stockings of regiments with the royal livery were usually blue.

Grenadiers. Each regiment of French infantry had grenadier companies in its battalions. The grenadier was equipped with grenade pouch and hatchet but it seems that few wore the sort or hat associated with grenadiers. Instead they wore the soft hat turned up at the sides, with the exception of the Gardes Francaises who had grenadier type hats.

THE CAVALRY

This period marks a considerable change in the standing of France's cavalry in Europe. At the start of the period the cavalry of Louis XIV were virtually unstoppable. During the War of the Grand Alliance this reputation continued and there were many famous exploits, but their tactics and operation did not move with the times and they failed to live up to their reputation in the War of the Spanish Succession. Their decline was epitomised by the demise of the squadrons of Gendarmerie at Blenheim. This section itemises the types of French cavalry, their uniform and equipment. They are divide into five types as follows:

Maison de Roi
Gensdarmes
Cavalerie Légère
Dragoons
Hussars

Maison du Roi. The cavalry of the Maison du Roi has already been covered. To recap it consisted of Mousquetaires, Gendarmes de la Garde, Gardes du Corps, Grenadiers a Cheval and Chevaux-Legers.

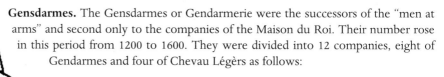

Gensdarmes. The Gensdarmes or Gendarmerie were the successors of the "men at arms" and second only to the companies of the Maison du Roi. Their number rose in this period from 1200 to 1600. They were divided into 12 companies, eight of Gendarmes and four of Chevau Légèrs as follows:

Gendarmes Écossais
Gendarmes Anglais
Gendarmes Bourguignons
Gendarmes de Flandre
Gendarmes and Chevaux Légers de la Reine
Gendarmes and Chevaux Légers du Dauphin
Gendarmes and Chevau Léger d'Anjou
Gendarmes and Chevaux Léger d'Orleans

In 1690 four more companies added.

Gendarmes and Chevau Léger de Bourgogne (became Bretagne in 1704)
Gendarmes and Chevau Leger de Berry

The Gendarmerie were dressed and equipped as for the Cavalerie Légère, which will be covered next. They wore scarlet coats, breeches and schabraque with pistol covers. The waistcoats were probably buff for all. The hat, tricorn style, was black edged silver for all companies. Later in the late century the colour of cross belt indicated the company but it is not clear if this held true for this period. The colours were Écossais - yellow; Anglais - violet; Bourguignons - dark green; Flandres - leaf brown; Gendarmes de la Reine - dark red; Chevau Légers de la Reine - dark red; Gendarmes Dauphins - dark blue; Chevaux Légers Dauphins - dark blue; Gendarmes d'Anjou - dark green; Chevaux Légers d'Anjou - dark aurore; Gendarmes d'Orleans - aurore; Chevaux Légers d'Orleans - aurore; Gendarmes Bourgogne - dark yellow; Chevaux Légers Bourgogne - dark violet; Gendarmes de Berry - dark red.

Cavalerie Légère. The third and largest category of French cavalry was the cavalerie légère. This was not light cavalry but corresponded to the Horse of the English army. In 1678 there had been 99 such regiments. The colour grey was already the dominant colour although there was no standardisation. The cuirass had been abolished in 1672 with the exception of the Cuirassier du Roi and for officers. The dress of the cavalerie légère was, in the 1680s, a broad brimmed felt hat turned up at the front or sides, a thick coat or *justscorps* with large sleeves, a waistcoat probably both of leather, breeches and high boot. A saddlecloth or schabraque, pistol covers and a cape rolled behind the saddle. No helmet was worn although a metal pot was worn inside or outside the hat. The armament was a sword, musket or muskotoon, cartridge box and a brace of pistols. The musket was suspended form a shoulder belt while the sword hung from a waistbelt and frog probably worn under the coat, which hung open. The dress of the Cavalerie Légère was brought into line in 1690. Details of some regiments are given in a separate table however in basic colours the dress of the 116 existing regiments at the time is given in the following list, taken from Susane's "Histoire de la Cavalerie".

Grey with red reverses: (87 regiments) Colonel Général, Mestre de camp general, Commissaire general, la Reine, Orleans, Chartres, Condé, Engheim, Tilladet, Arnolfini, Bartillat, La Valette, Grignan, Quinson, Saint Aignan, Du Gas, Crillon, Servon, Schomberg, Florensac, Varennes, chavalier Duc, Saint-Sylvestre, Heudicourt, Villeneuve, Saint-Valery, Gournay, Locmaria, Esclainvilliers, Villars, du Bordage, Melac, Villeroy, Lumbres, Tallard Villacerf, Pelleport, Montgommery,

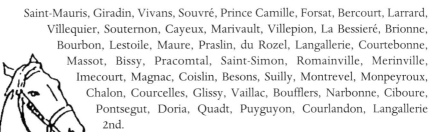

Saint-Mauris, Giradin, Vivans, Souvré, Prince Camille, Forsat, Bercourt, Larrard, Villequier, Souternon, Cayeux, Marivault, Villepion, La Bessieré, Brionne, Bourbon, Lestoile, Maure, Praslin, du Rozel, Langallerie, Courtebonne, Massot, Bissy, Pracomtal, Saint-Simon, Romainville, Merinville, Imecourt, Magnac, Coislin, Besons, Suilly, Montrevel, Monpeyroux, Chalon, Courcelles, Glissy, Vaillac, Boufflers, Narbonne, Ciboure, Pontsegut, Doria, Quadt, Puyguyon, Courlandon, Langallerie 2nd.

Grey white coat with red reverses: (1 Regiment) Aubusson La Fenillade.

Grey coat with blue reverses: (4 Regiments). Souastre, Chatelot, Comte de Bissy, Chastelet 2nd.

Blue coat with red reverses. (13 Royal Regiments) Royal, le Roi, Royal Etranger, Cuirassier, Cravates, Royal Piedmont, Dauphin, Dauphin Etranger, Bourgogne, Royal-Allemand, Berry, Grand Royaux, Anjou.

Blue coat with blue reverses. (1 Royal Regiment) Royal-Roussilion.

Red coat with red reverses. (1 Regiment) de Noailles.

There were two French and seven foreign regiments for which details are not known. These were Rasseut and Fiennes; Royal Allemand 2nd, Quadt 2nd, Rottombourg, Legall, Manderschied, Furstemberg, and Geoffreville.

In Lienhart and Humbet (see bibliography) there is a plate purporting to show the cavalry according to the *Reglement* of 1st January 1690. This casts further light on some of the regiments mentioned but some of the information is contradictory. For example, five regiments are shown with red coats. These include the Irish regiment Fitz-James which was not formed until 1698, Pons only raised in 1689 and additionally Colonel Général and La Reine. De Noailles, agreeing with Susane, is the fifth regiment. Some other regiments are shown with black cuffs and facings which may well have came later. In all probability while some of the detail relates to 1690, some post dates the regulations. They appear very similar to those in the Zeughaus manuscript of 1761, although that is not to suggest they had not been in existence much longer. Despite this the list has been included as a table if only for the comparison and for the detail it provides on other items of dress.

The Cavalerie Légère after 1700 regularised the tricorn which replaced the broad rimmed felt hat turned up at the sides.

The number of the Cavalerie Légère fluctuated greatly; after the Peace of Ryswick in 1699 they were considerably reduced. Just two years later however, the disbanded units were reformed as well as many new ones being raised. During the war there were more than 135 regiments of horse and dragoons. In 1715 at the close of the war 58 regiments only of cavalerie légère and 15 of dragoons were retained

The Carabiniers. In 1690 all the regiments of cavalerie légère were established with a company of carabiniers. After Neerwinden, in 1693, these companies were formed into a single corps, the Royal Carabiniers, as they were named. They consisted of five brigades made up of 50 squadrons, each of two companies. They were dressed as cavalerie légère in blue coats with red facings and cuffs. They had buff breeches and waistcoat, blue saddlecloth and pistol housings, which were all laced with silver.

Dragoons. The dragoons served basically the same function in the French army that they did in other countries, that is mounted infantry. As one would therefore expect their arms, equipment and uniforms were similar in nature to their English counterparts.

By 1690 there were 31 regiments of dragoons. In this year new regulations set down the uniforms for the various regiments of dragoons. Of these the new uniforms for 15 regiments are not known. These 15 were Barbezieres, Pinsonnel, Chevilly, La Lande, Tesse, Catinat, Artois, Cilly, Valencay, Gevandan, Anvoile, Avaray, Verrue, Breteuil and Gobert. Suzane (see bibliography) gives the dress for the remaining 16. Leinhan and Humbert give a plate showing this information in more detail and unlike that of the cavalerie légère it conforms to other sources. The information is included in a table.

It would seem likely that these regulations remained operative throughout the War of the Spanish Succession and well beyond into the middle of the century although style and cut would have made some modifications. At the end of the war all but 15 regiments of dragoons were disbanded.

Hussars. It was in 1692 that hussars first made their appearance in the French Army. The hussar was to become a necessary ingredient of every European army by the second half of the 17th century. The first unit had two squadrons, each of three companies, commanded by a Hungarian in French service called Baron de Kronberg or Cornsberg. They were at first called Cornsberg then from 1693 Mortani. They were short lived and when Cornsberg fell into disgrace and left France in 1697 they ceased to exist. In 1701 the Elector of Bavaria gave King Louis a regiment of hussars. These were the Hussars Saint-Genies named after their colonel. They became Rattsky in 1707 and Lynden in 1743. Also in 1702 the Verseilles Hussars were formed from the remains of the Mortani Hussars who, on disbanding, had been absorbed by the Royal Allemand cavalry. The last hussar regiment of this period was Poldeack who were raised in Italy in 1706, became Filtz in 1706 and Monteils in 1707. In 1709 they were transferred to Spanish service. None of the hussar regiments achieved a permanent place in the French Army, that distinction going to Bercheny formed in 1720.

The uniform and dress of the hussars has always been exotic and flamboyant. The Hungarians had shaven heads with a scalp lock or ponytail falling to one side and also wore long drooping moustaches. The Saint Genies Hussars' dolman was sky blue with braid across the chest and tin buttons. The cuffs were small and red. Breeches were red with sky blue overalls. Hungarian boots were tan. The waist sash was yellow and the pelisse was a wolf skin worn over the shoulder. They wore a red bag type hat with a surrounding of fur. Feathers were frequently worn in the hat. They wore a simple bag or sabretache and the schabraque was sky blue with a fur saddle. The arms included pistols, axe or mace, carbine slung on a shoulder belt and a sabre suspended from the waist.

Cavalry Musicians. All cavalry regiments except hussars had drums and hautbois (similar to a fife) or trumpets. With the exception of the Grenadiers a Cheval and the dragoons, which had a side drum, all the other regiments had kettle drummers. These were held in great esteem and drums were regarded as trophies of war. The kettledrummers generally wore the royal livery or a liverie based on the regimental colour. Their appearance was quite magnificent. By 1720 some kettledrummers were negros. It would appear that dragoons had hautbois while the cavalerie légère and Gendarmerie had trumpets. An illustration of a musician with hautbois of the Languedoc dragoons in 1720 shows a blue coat with red cuffs, waistcoat and breeches with silver lace. Hautbois players may not have worn livery, whereas illustrations of several trumpeters of the cavalerie légère at the same time show them in elaborate livery of the same style as the kettledrummers. This suggests that dragoon drummers may not have worn a livery either, at this time, although the drummers of the Grenadiers a Cheval wore livery.

THE ARTILLERY

In 1668 six companies of *canonniers* were formed, followed quickly by another six. In 1671 the Regiment des Fusiliers du Roi were raised to guard the artillery. The organisation gradually grew so that by 1677 there were six battalions. Disbanded in 1679 they were re-establishes in 1691. Meanwhile in 1684 the Regiment Royal des Bombardiers were formed as one battalion of 12 companies. In 1693 the Fusiliers du Roi were renamed Regiment Royal de l'Artillerie. Two years later the companies of canonniers were incorporated in the regiment. Finally, by 1701 the regiment consisted of five battalions, each of 13 companies (two of canonniers, two were fusiliers and one of *ouvriers* or artificers). At the same time a second battalion of Royal des Bombardiers were raised and the two battalions named Le Corps d'Artillerie.

Civilians drove the train at this time, the guns were brass or bronze and their carriages are givens in one source as blue, in another red. The uniforms of the above troops during this period were red breeches and stocking with a black tricorn, yellow lace and white rosette. The buttons were yellow. Canonniers wore blue coats, red cuffs and breeches, red waistcoat and stockings. They had a black hat with yellow trim. Royal de Bombardiers in 1710 wore red coat with blue cuffs, lining, waistcoat and stockings and a grenadier type hat of cloth.

GENERAL STAFF

Not until 1724 were regulations produced for the French general staff which stipulated a coat of blue with varying degrees of gold lace. From pictures of the time one may assume that this was the general rule prior to this date although portraits of general officers are not particularity helpful. The reason for that is that pictures were painted with the subject in armour although this was not normally worn, even in battle. In general officers wore fine clothes, perhaps with jackets of brown, various shades of blue or red with elaborate gold or silver lace, military orders and sword on a waist belt or baldric. The hat adapted in step with fashion until it became the tricorn, elaborately laced and plumed.

Illustrations

FRENCH HORSE AND DRAGOONS 1690

FRENCH CAVALRY 1690

REGIMENT	Coat	Cuffs	Facing	W/coat	Breeches	Hat Lace	Buttons	Shabraque
Royal	Blue	Red	Red	Buff	Buff	Yellow	Yellow	Blue edged aurora
de ROI	Blue	Blue	Red	Buff	Buff	Yellow	Yellow	Blue edged blue/white/red
Dauphin	Blue	Red	Red	Buff	Buff	Yellow	Yellow	Blue edged aurora
Colonel -general	Red	Black	Red	Buff	Buff	Yellow	Yellow	Red edged black/white
La Reine	Red	Blue	Red	Buff	Buff	Yellow	Yellow	Red edged white
Noailles	Red	Red	Red	Buff	Buff	Yellow	Yellow	Red edged white
Pons	Red	Blue	Red	Buff	Buff	White	White	Blue edged white
Fitzjames	Red	Green	Red	Buff	Buff	White	White	Red edged white
Commissaire -General	Grey/White	Black	Grey/White	Buff	Buff	White	White	Red edged white
Mestre de Camp General	Grey/White	Black	Grey/White	Buff	Buff	White	White	Red edged buff
Conty	Grey/White	Red	Grey/White	Buff	Buff	White	White	Red edged white

FRENCH DRAGOONS REGULATION OF 1690

REGIMENT	Coat	Cuff	Collar	Lining	W/Coat	Breeches	Bonnet Bag	Bonnet Surround	Saddle
Colonel General	Red	Blue	Red	Blue	Blue	Blue	Blue	Red	Blue edged white
Mestre-de-Camp General	Red	Blue	Red	Blue	Blue	Red	Blue	Red	Blue edged white
Royal	Blue	Red	Blue	Red	Red	Blue	Red	Brown fur	Red edged white
La Reine	Red	Red	Red	Red	Red	Blue	Red	Brown fur	Red edged white
Dauphin	Blue	Red	Blue	Red	Red	Blue	Red	Brown fur	Red edged white
R.Grammont	Red	Isabelle	Red	Isabelle	Isabelle	Red	Isabelle	Brown fur	Isabelle edged white
Languedoc 1st	Red	Red	Red	Red	Red	Blue	Red	Brown fur	Red edged white
Languedoc 2nd	Red	Red	Red	Red	Red	Blue	Red	Brown fur	Red edged white
Fontbeausard	Red	Yellow	Red	Yellow	Yellow	Red	Yellow	Brown fur	Yellow edged white
M.De Grammont	Red	Green	Red	Green	Green	Red	Green	Brown fur	Green edged white
Boufflers	Green	Green	Green	Green	Green	Red	Green	Brown fur	Green edged white
Asfeld	Red	Lime Green	Red	Lime Green	Lime Green	Red	Lime Green	Brown fur	Lime green edged white
Wentigny	Red	Yellow	Red	Yellow	Yellow	Red	Yellow	Brown fur	Yellow edged white
Spully	Red	Red	Red	Red	Red	Red	Red	Brown fur	Red edged white
D'Asfeld	Green	Red	Green	Red	Red	Red	Red	Brown fur	Red edged white
Fimarcon	Green	Green	Green	Green	Green	Red	Green	Brown fur	Green edged white

FRENCH FOOT

REGIMENT	Coat	Collar	Cuffs	W/Coat	Breeches	Hat Lace	Buttons	Button Arrangement Pocket Cuff		Pocket	Remarks
Gardes Francais	Blue	White	Red	Red	Red	Silver	Silver	5	3	Upright	Stockings red. White lace in groups of three.
Gardes Suisses	Red		Blue	Blue	Blue	White	White	5	3	Cross	Stockings blue. White lace in groups of three.
Picardie	Grey/White	Grey/White	Grey/White	Red	White	Yellow	Yellow	9	-	Upright	
Champagne	Grey/White	Grey/White	Grey/White	Red	White	Yellow	Yellow	6	5	Double Upright	
Piedmont	Grey/White	Grey/White	Grey/White	Grey/White	White	Yellow	Yellow	3	3	Cross	Red stockings. Officer/NCOs black cuffs
Navarre	Grey/White	-	Grey/White	Grey/White	White	Yellow	Yellow	7	5	Cross	
Normandie	Grey/White	Grey/White	Grey/White	Grey/White	White	White	White	3	3	Cross	Officers/NCOs Black cuffs
La Marine	Grey/White	Black	Black	Red	White	Yellow	Yellow	3	3	Cross	
Auxerrois	White		Red			White	White	3	3	Cross	Pocket demi ecusson
Bourbonnais	White	White	White	White	White	Yellow	Yellow	6	4	Double Upright	Buttons in pairs
Rambures, Feugueleres, Leuville	White	Red	White	White	White	Yellow	Yellow	3	3	Cross	5 buttons on lapel, 4 buttons below, white cloth had a blue tint
Auvergne	Grey/White	Grey/White	Grey/White	White	White	Yellow	White	3	3	Cross	
Sault, Tesse (1703), Talard	Grey/White	Violet	Violet	White	White	Yellow	Yellow	3	3	Cross	

Regiment											Notes
Espagny, Bandeville, Nettancourt,	Grey/White	White	White	White	White	Yellow	Yellow	3	3	Upright	
Royal	Grey/White	Royal Blue	Royal Blue	Royal Blue	Royal Blue	Yellow	Yellow	5	3	Double Upright	
Artois	Grey/White	Grey/White	Grey/White	Grey/White	Grey/White	Yellow	Yellow	3	8	Upright	Pocket en ecusson
Poitou	Grey/White	Royal Blue	Royal Blue	Royal Blue	White	Yellow	Yellow	6	4	Upright	Red stockings
Lyonnais	Grey/White	White	Red	Green	White	Yellow	Yellow	3	3	Double Upright	
Crussol, Gondrin, Leqervasais	Grey/White	Red	Grey/White	Red	White	White	White	6	5	Cross	Red stockings
Tourain	Grey/White	Blue	Blue	Blue	White	White	White	3	4	Double Upright	
Anjou	Grey/White	Royal Blue	Royal Blue	Royal Blue	Royal Blue	Yellow	Yellow	5	4	Cross	Royal Blue stockings
Maine	Grey/White	Blue	Blue	Blue	White	Yellow	Yellow	3	3	Upright	
Dampierre, D'humieres, Saillant,	Grey/White	Green	Green	White	White	Yellow	Yellow	7	3	Cross	
Coetquen, 1702 Tourville	Grey/White	Red	Red	Red	White	Yellow	Yellow	6	3	Double Upright	Cuff buttons in pairs. Red stockings
Grancey, La Chesnelaye	White	Red	Red	White	White	Yellow	Yellow	3	3	Cross	
La Reine	White	Red	Red	Blue	White	White	White	8	3	Cross	Pockets en ecusson. Red stockings
Limousin	White	Red	Red	Red	White	Yellow	Yellow	4	4	Cross	
Bourbon	White	Red	Red	Red	White	White	White	9	5	Upright	
Royal des Vaisseaux	Grey/White	Blue	Blue	Red	White	Yellow	Yellow	3	3	Double Upright	
Orleans	White	Red	Red	Red	White	Yellow	Yellow	4	3	Cross	Red stockings
La Couronne	Grey/White	Blue	Blue	Blue	White	White	White	3	3	Cross	Blue stockings
Bretagne	White	White	White	Red	Red	Yellow	Yellow	3	3	Upright	
Perch	Grey/White	White	Red	White	White	White	White	3	3	Upright	
Conde	White	White	Red	Red	White	Yellow	Yellow	5	5	Cross	
Saint Sulpice, Lannoy Louvignies	White	Red	Red	Red	White	White	White	3	3	Cross	
Vendome, Berry, Barrois (1714)	White	Blue	Blue	Blue	White	White	White	3	3	Cross	
La Sarre	White	Blue	Blue	Red	White	Yellow	Yellow	3	3	Cross	
La Fere	White	Red	Red	White	White	White	White	3	3	Cross	
Alsace	Turquin Blue	Red	Red	White	White	White	White	5	0	Cross	Red lining and lapels. Blue very pale
Royal Roussillon	White	Blue	Blue	Blue	White	Yellow	Yellow	3	6	Cross	
Dauphin	Grey/White	Royal Blue	Royal Blue	Royal Blue	White	Yellow	Yellow	9	0	Double Upright	36 small buttons on w/coat 14 buttons on coat
Beauvoisis	White	White	White	Red	White	White	White	6	3	Double Upright	
Rouergue	White	Red	Red	Red	White	Yellow	Yellow	3	3	Cross	Red stockings
Bourgogne	Grey/White	Grey/White	White	Red	White	Yellow	Yellow	3	3	Cross	
Royal La Marine	White	White	Royal Blue	Royal Blue	Royal Blue	White	White	3	3	Cross	
Vermandois	White	Red	Red	Blue	White	Yellow	Yellow	6	3	Double Upright	Pocket buttons in pairs
Furstemberg, Greder	Light Blue	White	Yellow	White	Blue	White	White	3	3	Double Upright	German-yellow lining 8 buttons on lapels and 12 on w/coat
Erlach Manuel Villars-Chandieu	Red	Red	Royal Blue	Red	Royal Blue	White	White	3	3	Large Cross	Swiss - blue lace button holes on pockets. White lace loops and buttonholes on w/coat. NCOs blue coat with red collar, cuffs and laced w/coat.
Stuppa, Brendle	Red	Medium Blue	Medium Blue	Medium Blue	Medium Blue	White	White	3	0	Cross	Swiss-blue lace loops on pockets
Salis-Sizers, Porlier, Reinold	Red	Medium Blue	Medium Blue	Medium Blue	Medium Blue	White	White	3	3	Cross	Swiss-blue lace button holes on w/coat
Pfyffer, Hessy,	Red	Red	Blue	Blue	Blue	White	White	3	3	Cross	Swiss-blue lace loops on left side of coat and pocket. Blue lace button holes on w/coat
Languedoc	White	Light Blue	Light Blue	Light Blue	White	Yellow	Yellow	6	3	Cross	Red stockings
Huxelles, Do Plessis-Bellieres, Montsoreau, Sourches	White	White	White	Red	White	Yellow	Yellow	5	5	Cross	

Greder Affry	Red	Light Blue	Light Blue	Yellow (another source blue)	Light Blue	White	White	3	3	Cross	Swiss
Medoc (from 1691)	White	Red	Red	Red	White	White	White	3	3	Cross	
D'Albret, Gandelus, Clerembault, Mirabeau, Gensac	White	Red	Red	Red	White	Yellow	Yellow	5	5	Cross	Red stockings
Castries, Morangies, Louvigny Bacqueville Vexin in 1762	White	Black	Red	Red	White	Yellow	Yellow	6	3	Double Upright	
Royal Comtois	White	White	Royal Blue	Royal Blue	White	Yellow	Yellow	9	3	Double Upright	
Schomberg, Larray, Sceaux, Lyonne	White	White	White	White	White	Yellow	Yellow	5	5	Cross	
Provence	White	Red	Red	Red	White	Yellow	Yellow	4	8	Cross	NCOs wore a red uniform edged in gold lace. Hat and cuffs edged silver.
Stuppa, Surbeck, Hemel	Red	Red	Light Blue	Light Blue	Light Blue	White	White	3	3	Cross	Swiss - Light blue lace, loops on coat white lace loops and buttonholes on w/coat.
Konigsmark, La Marck in 1693	Light Blue	Yellow	Yellow	Light Blue	Light Blue	White	White	3	3	Cross	German - Light blue lining. White lace buttonholes on coat and w/coat.
Toulouse	White	Light Blue	Light Blue	Light Blue	White	White	White	3	3	Cross	
Boulonnais	White	Light Blue	Light Blue	Light Blue	White	Yellow	Yellow	8	4	Cross	
Angoumois	White	Red	White	Light Blue	White	White	White	3	3	Cross	
Perigord	White	Red	Light Blue	Red	White	Yellow	White	3	3	Cross	
Saintonge	White	Light Blue	Light Blue	Light Blue	White	White	Yellow	3	3	Cross	
Foix	White	Red	Red	Light Blue	White	Yellow	Yellow	3	3	Cross	
Quercy	White	Red	Red	Red	White	Yellow	Yellow	5	5	Cross	
Jeune-Salis, May, Du Bulsson	Red	Medium Blue	Medium Blue	Medium Blue	Medium Blue	White	White	4	3	Cross	Swiss - Blue lace button holes on pocket, w/coat edged white lace with 11 loops each side. 4 loops on w/coat pocket.
Courten	Red	Red	Medium Blue	Medium Blue	Medium Blue	White	White	3	3	Cross	Swiss - Blue lace button holes on w/coat
Lee, Bulkeley	Red	Black	Black	Red	White	Yellow	Yellow	3	3	Cross	Irish - White lining and black lapels. 7 buttons on w/coat.
Lee, Talbot, Clare, O'Brien	Red	White	Yellow	Red	White	White	White	4	4	Cross	Irish - Yellow lining white lace on w/coat button holes. White epaulette. 12 buttons in pairs on coat
Liesler, Sparre, Lenck, in 1742 Royal Suedois	Medium Blue	Medium Blue	Chamois Yellow	Medium Blue	Grey/Black	Yellow	Yellow	3	3	Upright	German - Originally Swedish grey/black stockings.
Chartres	White	Red	Red	Red	White	Yellow	Yellow	5	3	Cross	
Barrois	White	Red	Medium Blue	Red	White	White	White	3	3	Cross	
Dorington, Roth in 1719	Red	Red	Medium Blue	Medium Blue	Medium Blue	Yellow	Yellow	3	3	Cross	Irish - Blue lining. 12 buttons down front of coat, 3 aurora lace button holes on pocket, 12 on the w/coat. 3 aurora loops on cuff.
Enghien, 1708 Mercy	Grey/White	Grey/White	Red	Red	Red	White	White	3	3	Cross	Formed 1706 but details are 1720. Lining and stockings red.
Royal Baviere	Medium Blue	Black	Black	Medium Blue	Medium Blue	White	White	4	0	Cross	German - Black lapels, white lining, 10 buttons on coat and w/coat laced with white.
Thiangers, Duc de 1702 Mortemart, Duc de	White	Red	Red	Red	White	Yellow & white	Yellow & white	3	3	Cross	Buttons placed alternately 1 yellow between 2 white

Dutch Infantry Officer No 19 Salm, later Dohna Ferassieres

© Bob Marrion 2004

French - Infantry, Regiment Louvigny

© Bob Marrion 2004

French - Irish Regiment, O'Brien c.1712
(by H Boisselier)

French - Irish Regiment, Dorrington c.1710

(by H Boisselier)

Name											Notes
Isenghien	White	Red	Red	White	White	Yellow	Yellow	3	3	Cross	W/coat had red lapels
Nice	White	White	White	Red	White	Yellow	Yellow	3	3	Upright	
Guyenne	White	Red	Red	Red	White	Yellow	Yellow	3	3	Cross	
Lorraine,	White	Red	White	White	White	White	White	3	3	Upright	
Flandres,	White	Light blue	Light blue	Light blue	White	Yellow & white	Yellow & white	4	3	Cross	1st and 3rd buttons yellow on pockets, middle button yellow on cuff, coat alternate
Berry	White	Red	Red	Red	White	Yellow	Yellow	3	5	Double upright	
Bearn	White	Red	Red	Red	White	Yellow	Yellow	4	4	Double upright	Red stockings
Haynaut	White	Red	Red	Red	White	Yellow	Yellow	3	3	Cross	
Bigorre	White	Light blue	Light blue	Light blue	White	Yellow	Yellow	3	3	Cross	
Bresse	White	Light blue	Light blue	Light blue	Light blue	Yellow	Yellow	6	6	Cross	collar very small, yellow lace button holes on coat, pocket & w/coat
Lamarche,	White	White	Red	Red	White	Yellow	Yellow	5	5	Cross	
Brie,	White	Red	Red	Red	White	Yellow	Yellow	9	3	Upright	
Soissonnais	White	Light blue	Light blue	Light blue	White	Yellow	Yellow	3	3	Cross	
Isle de France	White	Light blue	Light blue	Light blue	White	Yellow	Yellow	3	3	Double upright	
Forez	White	Red	?	Red	White	Yellow	Yellow	3	3	Cross	
Cambresis,	White	Red	Red	Red	White	Yellow	Yellow	9	-	Cross	
Tournaisis,	White	Red	Red	Red	White	Yellow	Yellow	5	-	Cross	Small buttons
Nivernais	White	Light blue	Light blue	Light blue	White	White	White	4	4	Cross	
Vexin	White	White	Light blue	White	White	Yellow	Yellow	5	3	Cross	
Aunis	White	White	Red	White	White	Yellow	Yellow	5	3	Cross	
Beauce	White	White	Red	White	White	Yellow	Yellow	4	3	Double upright	
Dauphine	White	White	Medium Blue	White	White	White	Yellow	3	3	Cross	
Vivarais	White	White	Red	Red	White	Yellow	Yellow	5	3	Cross	Pockets demi ecusson
Luxembourg	White	Medium Blue	Medium Blue	Medium Blue	White	White	White	4	3	Cross	
Bassigny	White	White	Medium Blue	Dark Red	White	Yellow	Yellow	4	3	Cross	
Beaujollis	White	White	Red trimmed yellow	White	White	Yellow	Yellow	5	3	Upright	
Pontieu	White	White	Red	White	White	White	White	3	3	Cross	
Colonels, de Solre 1711 de Boufflers 1712 Delavalllere	White	White	Red	White	White	Yellow	Yellow	6	5	Upright	
Colonels, 1689 de Tesse, 1703 de Ssuzay, I716 D'olonne.	White	White	Red	White	White	Yellow	Yellow	3	3	Cross	
Colonels, 1691 Noalles, 1704 de Beaufferme, 1708 Perrin, 1719 Montfort	White	White	Red	White	White	White	White	4	3	Cross	
1694 Colonels Lee, 1733 Bulkeley.	Red	Red	Dark Green	Dark Green	Dark Green	White	White	3	3	Cross	Irish: all button holes laced yellow
Blaisos	White	White	Red	Red	White	White	White	4	3	Upright	
Gatinais,	White	White	Red	Red	White	White	White	4	3	Upright	
Auxerrois	White	White	Red	Red	White	White	White	3	3	Cross	Pockets demis ecusson
Agenois	White	White	Red	White	White	White	White	4	6	Upright	
Santerre	White	White	Blue	White	White	Yellow	Yellow	4	3	Cross	
Des Landes	White	White	White	White	White	Yellow	Yellow	3	3	Cross	
Berwick 1702 - 1715	Red	White	Yellow	Yellow	Yellow	Yellow	Yellow	6	4	Double upright	Irish: buttons in pairs, 24 on w/coat, white lining. All button holes lace yellow
Conte de Chardlois	White	Red	Red	Red	White	White	White	5	5	Double upright	
Albaret	White	White	White	White	White	White	White				
Baudeville	White	White	White	White	White	White	White				
Royal Italien	Brown	Brown	Red	Red	Red	Yellow	Yellow	3	3	Cross	Italian: red lining & stockings

THE PRUSSIAN ARMY

BACKGROUND

The army of Brandenburg-Prussia inherited by Frederick III in 1688 was a well trained one with a high degree of uniformity for the time. Centralised power and control rested with the Elector who was commander in chief. The army's administration was sound and it had won the respect of the other European powers. Whatever the other weaknesses of the Great Elector's son, and despite the scorn caused by his love of the ceremonial, he continued to build and improve the army.

In the War of the Grand Alliance Brandenburg-Prussia played her part on the side of the allies. For his support in the War of the Spanish Succession Frederick became, with the Hapsburg agreement, Frederick I King of Prussia in 1701. The Prussian field army was commanded by Prince Leopold von Anhalt Dessau. Throughout the war the Prussian army improved, distinguishing itself at Blenheim, Turin and Malplaquet in particular. Crown Prince Frederick William seeing the results at the latter battle, returned to Prussia to sponsor further improvements to the army. When the Crown Prince took over the throne on the death of his father in 1715 he inherited a very good army, which was to make its mark on Europe in the ensuing years.

THE INFANTRY

In 1685 Prussia had six infantry regiments, but by 1700 there were 18 and in 1715 there were 27. In 1691 the Elector ordered all guard battalions to be uniformed in blue with white distinctions. The remainder were to be in blue lined red. In 1700 the Grenadier-Garde wore blue grenadier coat with white collar, cuffs and lapels, a blue waistcoat lined white and blue breeches and white stockings. The coats had become tailored except for the grenadiers who retained the looser open coat turned back at the front. The grenadier cap had a white face coming to a point with crimson ornamentation. The surround was white and the bag crimson with a white tassel. Belts were buff and the large cartridge box was white with crimson cypher and ornaments. Officers wore crimson coats, hats with heavy gold lace and black stockings. The infantry coat was more tailored at the waist except for grenadiers who retained the full, open style coat. Stockings for the infantry were generally red. The elkskin waistcoat had been, or was, being, replaced by waistcoats of cloth.

The Leibgarde zu Fuss in 1705 wore blue coats lined and turned back with white, leather breeches and white stockings. NCOs had red coats, lined blue, with gold lace and officers, red coats, lined blue, with gold lace and black stockings. The black tricorn was edged gold with a white plume trim. In this year they became 'The Fusilier Guards' who were called 'White Guards'. By 1708 the 'White Guards' grenadiers wore a tall, pointed cap with black or dark blue front. On the front, at the base, was a white oval with black eagle and above it a gold plate with royal cypher in white. The grenadier's coat was open in the normal style, showing a dark blue waistcoat crossed with white lace at the button holes. The cartridge pouch was black with gold cypher and grenades in the corners. In the line regiments the degree of similarity imposed by the order to wear blue coats with red lining was circumvented to allow for regimental distinction. This was achieved by using different shades of red, different colours of waistcoat and breeches, and differing patterns of buttonhole lace in white. By the start of the War of the Spanish succession the pike had gone completely.

GARDE CAVALRY

The Trabant Leib Garde were formed in 1688 and wore a medium blue surtout over a buff coat with blue cuffs. The surtouts were edged and embroidered in gold. In the same year the Grand Mousqueteers wore crimson coats with gold lace. By 1699 the Garde du Corps were dressed in blue coats, (officers in red) with gold lace. The blue coats had large red (or crimson) cuffs edged gold and the buttonholes up the front of the coat were lace in gold. The cartridge belt had gold-crimson-gold-crimson-gold bands. Around the waist was a gold and crimson sash. The Gendarmes, formed from the Grand Mousqueteers, had blue coats with silver loops on the sleeves and silver lace buttonholes. They had blue cloth cloaks with gold lace collars and black hats, edged silver. In 1713 the Trabant Leib Garde were merged with the Gendarmes and the guard cavalry then consisted of the Garde du Corps.

THE HORSE

The horse were not cuirassiers, the cuirass having been set aside in the reign of Frederick I from 1688 to 1713 and did not return to service until 1736. The horse originally wore a buff colour coat with blue sleeves and white hoops about the arm. From illustrations made at the time it appears that a buff sleeveless jerkin was worn over the top, although this may be part of the coat. From about 1700 the buff colour was replaced by a coat of white or light grey. The carbine belt over the left shoulder was brown leather or regimental facing edged white. The troopers wore white or buff breeches and high black boots. The hat was of a black felt turned up on one or more sides and sources shows it edged. The schabraque, pistol covers and cloak roll were blue. Officers are shown in buff coats, lined blue with silver or white lace, yellow rosettes in their hats and gold lace on their horse furniture. Kettle drummers wore blue with gold lace, gold hoops on the arms of the coat and false sleeves edged and crossed in gold. By 1713 there were nine regiments of horse. In 1700 the officers generally wore red coats, but it is not clear when this ceased, there being no reference to it after this time. By default, one could assume that officers and NCOs in the horse generally subscribed to the uniform of the men but the uniform would be appropriately laced.

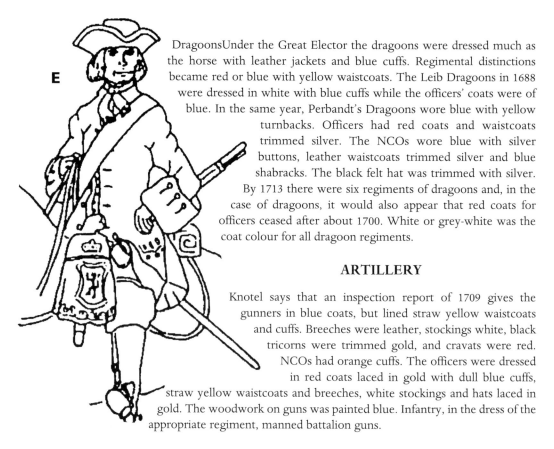

E

DragoonsUnder the Great Elector the dragoons were dressed much as the horse with leather jackets and blue cuffs. Regimental distinctions became red or blue with yellow waistcoats. The Leib Dragoons in 1688 were dressed in white with blue cuffs while the officers' coats were of blue. In the same year, Perbandt's Dragoons wore blue with yellow turnbacks. Officers had red coats and waistcoats trimmed silver. The NCOs wore blue with silver buttons, leather waistcoats trimmed silver and blue shabracks. The black felt hat was trimmed with silver. By 1713 there were six regiments of dragoons and, in the case of dragoons, it would also appear that red coats for officers ceased after about 1700. White or grey-white was the coat colour for all dragoon regiments.

ARTILLERY

Knotel says that an inspection report of 1709 gives the gunners in blue coats, but lined straw yellow waistcoats and cuffs. Breeches were leather, stockings white, black tricorns were trimmed gold, and cravats were red. NCOs had orange cuffs. The officers were dressed in red coats laced in gold with dull blue cuffs, straw yellow waistcoats and breeches, white stockings and hats laced in gold. The woodwork on guns was painted blue. Infantry, in the dress of the appropriate regiment, manned battalion guns.

Illustrations

A   Grenadier - Fusilier Leibgarde
B   Grenadier 1709
C   Leibgarde
D   Horse 1700
E   Dragoon 1710

PRUSSIAN HORSE AND DRAGOONS

REGIMENT

	Coat	Lining	Cuffs	W/coat	Breeches	Schabraque	Remarks
HORSE							
Hamel ,L'ostange, Portail	White	Scarlet	Scarlet	Leather	Leather	Scarlet edged white with scarlet edge	Black tricorn edged white
Markgraf Philipp Wilhelm	White	Bright Blue	Bright Blue	Leather	Leather	Bright blue edged white piped blue	Black tricorn edged silver, pouch bright blue, flap edged white silver buttons. Shoulder belt, white blue white
Kronprinz	Grey	Bright Blue	Bright Blue	Leather	Leather	Bright Blue edged White	Black tricorn edged silver
Schlippenbach	Grey/White	Deep Blue	Deep Blue	Buff	Buff	Deep blued edged white	Black tricorn edged silver. Tin buttons. In 1713 colour changed to red.
Leibregiment	Grey/White	Deep Blue	Deep Blue edged silver then gold in 1705	Deep blue	Buff	Deep blue edged white	Black tricorn edged silver until 1705 then gold
Heyden	Grey/White Deep blue	Deep Blue	Deep Blue	Deep blue	Leather	Deep blue edged white	Black tricorn edged white with black rosette, white buttons
Wartensleben	Grey/White	Green	Green	Green	Leather	Green edged White	Black tricorn edged white. Black rosette. White buttons.
Garde du Corps	Blue		Red edged Gold				Black tricorn edged gold. Carbine belt gold red gold red gold. Sword belt on other shoulder, buff. Gold buttons and lace on coat.
Gensdarmes	Blue					Blue	Silver loops on sleeves. Blue cloak with gold laced collar, black trim with silver lace.
Anhalt 1692 1713	White Grey/white	Blue Red	Blue Red		Leather	Blue edged White	
DRAGOONS							
Leibregiment	Grey/White	Blue	Blue	Blue	Leather	Blue edged white	Black tricorn edged silver. White buttons.
Sonsfeld	White	Red	Red	Red	Leather	Red edged white.	Black tricorn edged. Black rosette. White buttons
Markgraf Albrecht	White	Blue	Blue	Blue	Leather	Blue edged white	Black tricorn edged silver. Black rosette. White buttons.
Ansbach	White	Bright Blue	Bright Blue	Bright Blue	Leather	Blue edged white	Black tricorn edged silver. Black rosette. Yellow buttons.
Derfflingen	White	Red	Red	Red	Leather	Red edged white	Black tricorn edged silver. Black rosette. Yellow buttons
Lottum	Grey/White	Blue	Blue		Leather		Officers in red with silver lace.

PRUSSIAN FOOT

REGIMENT	Coat	Lining	Cuffs	W/coat	Breeches	Stockings	Remarks
Markgraf Christian Ludwig	Blue	Carmine Red	Carmine Red	Blue	Leather NCOs Blue. Officers Red	Red NCOs Blue. Officers Blue	Black tricorn edged white. White buttons Grenadier hat with red front, blue crown, yellow piping on surround white piping on crown.
Annalt Dessau	Blue	Red	Blue	Blue	Leather NCOs Blue. Officers Red	Red NCOs Blue. Officers Blue	Black tricorn edged yellow. Yellow buttons. Grenadier hat white front blue bag, white surround. Coloured crest on front.
Varenne	Blue	Red	Red	Red	Leather NCOs Blue. Officers Dark Blue	Blue NCOs Blue. Officers Dark Grey	Black tricorn edged white. White neck cloth.
Alt Dohna	Blue	Red	Red. Grenadier cuffs were . Blue	Red	Leather NCOs Blue. Officers Blue	Red NCOs Blue. Officers Dark Grey	Black tricorn edged yellow. Yellow buttons. White neck cloth. Grenadier hat red front, blue crown yellow piping and a grenade in front. White pompoms. Buff shoulder belt and back pouch.
Kronprinz	Blue	Red	Red, Blue for grenadiers	Blue	Leather NCOs Blue. Officers Blue	Red NCOs Blue. Officers Blue	Black tricorn edged yellow. Yellow buttons. Grenadier hat red front, blue crown, yellow piping.
Kanitz	Blue	White	Red	Blue	Red	Grey	Black tricorn with yellow edge and green sprig.
Leibregiment	Blue	White	White	Blue	Leather	White	Black tricorn edged white. Tin buttons. Officers red coats, w/coat & breeches. Grenadier cap red front and blue crown, yellow piping.
Donhoff	Blue	Red	Red	Red	Leather NCOs Red. Officers Red	Red NCOs Blue Officers Grey	Black edged white. Green sprig. White lace on buttonholes down coat, waistcoat on cuffs and pockets. Officers red coats.
Holstein-Beck	Blue	Red	Red	Red	Red	White NCOs Blue. Officers Dark Grey	Black tricorn with white edge and a green sprig of leaves. White buttons and buttonhole lace on coat, waistcoat pocket and cuffs.
Markgraf Albercht Van Brandenburg	Blue	Red	Red	Red	Leather NCOs Blue. Officers Red	Red NCOs Blue. Officers Grey	Black tricorn edged white. Yellow buttons. White neck cloth.
Anhal T Zerbst	Blue	Red	Red	Red	Leather NCOs Blue. Officers Blue	Red NCOs Blue. Officers Dark Grey	Black tricorn edged white. Yellow buttons
Fusiller-Leibgorde	Dark Blue	White turned all the way down front	White back	Dark blue with white bars of lace	Leather or Blue	White	Grenadier hat with dark blue front with white circle in bottom front and gold and white coat arms above it. Buff shoulder strap, black pouch edged gold with gold FR.
Van Schlagrendorff	Blue	Red Crimson	Red Crimson	Red Crimson	Red Crimson	Leather	Black tricorn edged yellow. White lace on jacket and waistcoat, buttons, button holes.

THE ARMIES OF THE GERMAN STATES

BACKGROUND

While Bavaria and Prussia have been dealt with separately due to their size and importance, there were many smaller German states that played a part in the war. Saxony was involved in all the wars in Eastern Europe, as indeed were some of the smaller states, but not the Spanish Succession. With these exceptions this section provides some information on the other German states.

In the late 17th and early 18th centuries the whole of what was later to become Germany was made up of a wide variety of principalities, kingdoms, bishoprics, duchies, free cities and so forth. In 1648 these were still loosely grouped under the Hapsburgs in the Holy Roman Empire. After the Peace of Westphalia at the end of the 30 Years War in 1648, the German states were devastated and exhausted by war. Also by this time the Austrian influence over the states had declined as the Hapsburgs centralised their power in southern Europe. In the years between the end of the war and the formation of the Grand Alliance the states recouped and recovered. Standing armies began to form and not infrequently these were beyond the needs and economies of their sponsors, not least in some German states. However, with the outbreak of war in 1689 these armies found employment either on behalf of their own masters or in the service of the larger allied powers. The German states were therefore heavily committed to both the War of the League of Augsburg and that of the Spanish Succession.

THE ARMIES

The separate uniform chart provides many details of a wide variety of regiments in a number of the German states. From the large number of states it will not be surprising that the uniforms are equally diverse and frequently subject to the whims of the small rulers. The charts cover the War of the Spanish Succession, however, in the notes that follow some earlier details have been included. The subject is a large one and little more than a general overview can be achieved here.

Anhalt. There were troops from Anhalt in the Imperial service in the 1680s and this continued in the next century. The infantry wore blue coats with red turn backs, red waistcoats and breeches with white stockings. The black felt hats had green ribbons. The horse furniture was blue lined red

Baden. There are few details other than white uniforms.

Brunswick. Knotel states that from 1697 the Brunswick infantry wore blue coats with red, yellow or white waistcoats and stockings to distinguish regiments. Blue also appears to have been the predominant colour for the horse and red for the dragoons.

Cologne. In 1702 the Cologne forces stood at six battalions of infantry (each regiment had two battalions) and 11 squadrons of cavalry. The Cologne uniforms were strongly influenced by those of both Bavaria and France. All coats were light blue for both infantry and cavalry. Black tricorns were decorated with a blue white cockade.

Hanover. The Hanoverian forces served with the Maritime powers and were either in Netherland or English pay. These totaled six battalions of infantry, eight squadrons of horse and three of dragoons in Netherland pay and eight battalions of infantry, six squadrons of horse and eight of dragoons in English pay. The Hanoverian infantry were usually dressed in red with distinguishing regimental facing colours. Hat lace was gold or silver corresponding to yellow or white buttons. With the exception of the *Leibgarde*, who wore red, the Hanoverian horse wore white with regimental colour distinctions. By 1700 the skirts of the coat were turned back producing the turnbacks, which were later to be military fashion throughout Europe. The cavalry hat was white felt until 1705 when the black tricorn was adopted. Breeches and waistcoats for both horse and dragoons were of bright yellow leather. Boots were brown at first then black. *Leib* companies wore bearskins. The cuirass was abolished in 1683. In 1706 officers wore yellow sashes over the right shoulder. Finally the artillery in 1700 wore red coats with blue cuffs and yellow lace, buff breeches and blue stockings.

Hessen-Darmstadt. Knotel gives details of the *Landausschuss*, a form of militia, which in 1700 was organised on the basis of a field army. The basic uniform was blue coats with regimental lining colour and with grey breeches and stockings. There was a *Leibgarde companie zu Pferd* that also wore dark blue coats with red. Details of quite a number of the foot regiments are given in the chart. There are several illustrations by Knotel, but these are dated 1717, rather beyond the specific period of the war.

Hessen-Kassel. The infantry of Hessen-Kassel wore blue while the horse wore grey.

Mecklenburg-Schwerin. The infantry started in grey uniforms then blue. Dragoons wore a grey white coat until 1705 then blue.

Palatinate. In 1688 there were three infantry regiments, one dragoon regiment and a guard cavalry and guard dragoon regiment. Before the war three more infantry and three cavalry were added. In 1701 another four infantry (in Dutch service) were raised and in 1702 a provincial infantry regiment. The troops of the Palatinate were generally dressed in various shades of blue for the infantry. Grenadiers wore a high felt mite cap with bag. The uniform style of the Palatinate lagged behind the European fashion. At the start of the war they were still equipped with matchlocks muskets which were replace with flintlock and plug bayonet during the first campaign, while the pike only left service in 1704. The horse wore grey except for the Lifeguards. The artillery in the war consisted only of battalion guns and the gunners were dressed as the fortress artillery with grey coats with carmine red cuffs.

Schwarzburg and Reuss. Schwarzburg and Reuss raised a foot regiment jointly for the War of the Spanish Succession. They were dressed in white with red cuffs but without collar and lapels.

Wurttemberg. In 1683 the *Leibgarde* infantry wore grey coats with yellow cuffs and waistcoats, buff breeches and grey stockings. *Leibgarde zu Pferd* were cuirassiers wearing yellow with red turnbacks and silver lace. In the same year the *Kreis Regiment Zu Pferd von Hohstedt* was raised in Swabia. It wore a blue grey coat with an unusual leather cuirass. This was still being worn in 1703. The artillery probably wore red.

REGIMENT	Coat	Lining	Cuffs	W/coat	Breeches	Schabraque	Remarks
COLOGNE							
Guard Hartshiere	Light Blue	Black	Black	Red	Light Blue	Light Blue edged silver?	Black edged silver
Carabinier Guard	Scarlet	White	Black	Buff	Buff		Hat edged silver
Guard Dragoons	Light Blue	White	White	White	White	Light Blue edged white?	
HANOVER							
Gardes du Corps	Red	Blue	Red, Blue from 1708	Straw	Buff	Red with silver border	Buttons and trim silver Bandolier blue trimmed silver
Reuther Liebregiment	Red	Blue	Blue	Buff	Buff	Blue with gold border	Hat white. Buttons Pewter Carbine strap red gold border
Croix de Frechappel/Schluter	White-grey	Light Blue	Light Blue	Buff	Buff	Light Blue white border	Hat black edged white
von Goden/ von Breidenbach	White/Grey	Sea Green	Sea Green	Buff	Buff	Sea Green edged white	Black edged yellow
Noyelles/ Schulenburg	White	Scarlet	Scarlet	Leather	Leather	Red edged white	Black tricorn edged silver. Red shoulder belt edged silver.
HESSE-KASSEL							
Erbach, 1705, Boyneburg	Grey/white	Bright green	Bright green	Leather	Leather	Bright green edged white	Black tricorn, no edging. White buttons
Spiegel	Grey	Blue	Blue	Blue	Leather	Blue	Black tricorn, no edging
Leibregiment	Grey	Red	Red	Red	Leather	Red	Black tricorn edged gold. Gold buttons.
HOLSTEIN GOTTORF							
Osten,1708 Grothusen	Blue with pale yellow lapel & colour	Pale Yellow	Pale Yellow	Leather	Leather	Blue edged pale yellow	Black tricorn no lace. Tin buttons. Lapel goes all the length of front
MUNSTER							
Nagel	White	Red	Red	Buff	Buff	Red edged White	Black tricorn edged white. White buttons
PALATINAT							
Venningen Gendarmes	Bright Grey	Deep Green	Deep Green	Bright Grey	Leather	Grey with Green edge	Black tricorn edged white. Black cuirass breastplate only worn over coat. Cuirass edged green.
Leibregiment	Indigo	Carmine	Carmine	Carmine	Leather	Blue edged white with blue piping Gold monogram on saddle & pistol caps	Black tricorn edged yellow. Drummer in reversed colours and white lace.
Wieser, 1706 Spee 1711 Mill	Ash Grey	Blue	Blue	Ash Grey	Leather	Ash Grey.	Black tricorn edged Drummer in reverse colours. White lace white. Tin buttons.
RHINE SUPERIOR							
Nassau - Weilburg	Ash Grey	Red	Red	Red	Leather	Ash Grey edged red	Black tricorn edged white. Green foliage. Black cravat, copper buttons. Red knot on right shoulder. Trumpeter in reversed colours
SWABIA							
Fugger	Grey	Grey	Red	Red	Grey	Red edged white	Leather cuirass. Black tricorn edged white with white rosette with black centre. White cravat. Trumpeter in reverse colours.
Wurttemberg	Grey	Grey	Grey	Sky Blue	Sky Blue	Blue edged white	Leather cuirass. Black tricorn as above. Trumpeter in yellow coat with black cuffs, w/coat lining and breeches. Gold lace.
WURTTEMBERG							
Leibgarde	Yellow	Red	Red piped yellow	Red	Red	Yellow edged black	Black tricorn edged gold with green foliage. Silver metal cuirass trimmed in red worn over coat, trumpeter in yellow and black.

DRAGOONS

ANSBACH

Schmettau	Bright Blue	Carmine	Carmine	Carmine	Leather	Carmine edged white	Tricorn edged white. White buttons.

BRUNSWICK

Volkening	Carmine		Deep Green		Leather	Carmine	Black tricorn edged gold with white cockade, gold buttons.

HANOVER

Villars	White	Red	Red	Leather	Leather	Red lined white	Black tricorn edged white. White buttons
Van Bothmer	White	Bright Blue	Bright Blue	Buff	Buff	Bright Blue	Black tricorn edged white. Tin buttons
Van Bulow	White	Deep Blue	Deep Blue	Buff	Buff	Deep Blue	Black tricorn edged yellow, yellow buttons. Drummer deep blue coat, white cuffs.

HESSEN-DARMSTADT

Prinz Franz Ernst Dragoons 1717	Green with red lapel	Red	Red	Buff	Buff	Green lined yellow	Black tricorn edged white

HESSEN-KASSEL

Erbprinz	Indigo Blue	Red	Red	Red	Leather	Deep Blue edged red	Black tricorn edged silver. White buttons. Drummer in reversed colours
Hessen-Homburg, 1704 Aurochs	White	Yellow	Yellow	Yellow	Leather	Yellow edged yellow and black	Black tricorn edged white. Silver buttons. Officer's coats red with yellow cuffs. Drummer red coat.

HOLSTEIN - GOTTORF

Baudissin	Blue	Blue	Blue	Blue		Blue edged white	Black tricorn, no lace. White buttons
Dernath	Blue	Red	Red	Blue		Blue edged white	Brown fur grenadier hat with small red plume on left side (fat all). Jacket and waistcoat edged in white lace with red pattern. Buttonholes also laced.

SWABIA

Franz Anton Van Hohenzollern-Sigmaringen	Grey	Black	Black	Black	Leather	Black edged hite	Black tricorn edged white with green foliage. White buttons. Drummer in reverse colours.

WURZBURG

Techenbach	Grey/white	Mid Blue	Mid Blue	Mid Blue	Leather	Blue edged white	Black tricorn edged white with green foliage. White cravat and buttons. Drummer in reversed colours.

GERMAN STATES - FOOT

REGIMENT	Coat	Lining	Cuffs	W/coat	Breeches	Stockings	Remarks
ANSBACH/BAYREUTH							
Heydrbrecht until 1705 Seckendorf Until 1711 then Cavenwach	Deep Blue	Carmine	Carmine	Carmine	Leather	Grey	Black tricorn edged white, white buttons. Drummers in carmine coat with white cuffs.
BRUNSWICK							
Erbprinz August Wilhelm	Deep Blue	Yellow	Yellow	Deep Blue	Leather	Yellow	Black tricorn edged yellow. Green leaves in hat, copper buttons. Drummers yellow coat, bright blue cuffs and lining
Bernstorff	Deep Blue	Carmine	Carmine	Carmine	Leather	Carmine	Black tricorn edged yellow. Green leaves in hat, copper buttons. Drummers yellow coat, bright blue cuff trimming
Bevern	Deep Blue	Deep Blue	Yellow, 1706 white	Deep Blue	Leather	Grey	Black tricorn edged white. Green leaves in hat.
COLOGNE							
Foot Guards	Light Blue	Red	Red	White	White	Black	Hat edged white
Bernsau	Light Blue	Rose	Rose	White	White	Black	Hat edged yellow
St.Maurice	Light Blue	White	White	White	White	Black	Hat edged white
Trabant Guard	Light Blue	Black	Black	Light Blue	Light Blue	Red	Hat was white edged silver
HANOVER							
Leib Infantry Regiment	Red	Black	Black	Red	Buff	White	Hat edge and button holes yellow
De Charles	Red	Dark Green	Dark Green	Straw	Buff	White	Hat edged white
Benstorff	Red	White	White	White	Buff	White	Hat edged yellow
De Luc	Pre 1706 White	Green	Green	Staw yellow	White	White	Hat edged white
	1706 Red	Straw	Straw	Straw	White	White	Hat edged yellow, brass buttons
La Motte	Carmine	Bright Blue	Bright Blue	Bright Blue	Bright Blue	White	Black tricorn edged white. White buttons. Drummers reverse colours
HESSEN DARMSTADT							
Schrautenbach	Deep Blue	Red	Red	Red	Deep Blue	Grey	Black tricorn edged white. White buttons. Grenadier cap blue front, red bag. Lion rampant on front and red and white horizontal stripes
HESSEN-KASSEL							
Prince Carl till 1703, Prince Leopold till 1705, Prince Ludwig till 1706, Prince Max	Indigo Blue	Yellow	Blue	Blue	Leather	White with blue spots	Black tricorn no lace. Drummer in green with yellow cuffs, waistcoat and breaches. Gold lace.
Grenadiers	Indigo Blue	Red	Red	Red	Leather	Red	Grenadier cap, high fronted in red with red bag and white piping.
Lowenstein, 1703 Stockrad	Indigo Blue	Bright Red	Bright Red	Blue	Leather	Grey	Black tricorn edged yellow. Yellow buttons
Wartensleben, 1709 Prince Georg	Indigo Blue	Indigo Blue	Indigo Blue	Indigo Blue	Leather	Grey	Black tricorn no edging. Yellow buttons
Leibregiment	Indigo Blue	White	White	Indigo Blue	Indigo Blue	White	Black tricorn no edging. Yellow buttons
Anhalt - Bernburg	Indigo Blue	Yellow	Yellow	Indigo Blue	Leather	Yellow	Black tricorn no edging. Copper buttons. Drummers green coat.
Schopping	Indigo Blue	White	White	White	Leather	Grey	Black tricorn no edging. Yellow buttons
Erbprinz	Indigo	Red	Red	Red	Leather	Red	Black tricorn no edging. White buttons. Drummers reverse colours white lace.
HOLSTEIN GOTTORF							
Van Adercass, 1708 Van Grothusen	Carmine with orange lapels	Orange	Orange	Carmine	Leather	Grey	Black tricorn no edging. White buttons and cravat. Lapel the length of coat.
Barner	Carmine with blue lapels	Blue	Blue	Carmine	Leather	Grey	Black tricorn no edging. White buttons and cravat. Lapel the length of coat.
Dobrokoffsky	Carmine with white lapels	White	White	Carmine	Leather	Grey	Black tricorn no edging. White buttons and cravat. Lapel the length of coat.

MECKLENBURG SCHWERIN							
Schwerin	Deep Blue	Deep Blue	Red	Deep Blue	Deep Blue	Red	Black tricorn edged yellow. White cravat.
MUNSTER							
Nagel	Grey	Red	Red	Grey	Grey	Grey	Black tricorn edged white. White buttons Drummers in reverse colours.
OSNABRUCK							
Spiegal	Grey/white	Green	Green	Green	Green	Green	Black tricorn edged yellow. White cravat, yellow buttons. Drummers in reverse colours
Leibregiment	Bright Green	White	White	White	White	White	Black tricorn with green foliage. White cravat and buttons. Drummer red coat with green cuffs, lining w/coat and breeches. Red stockings.
PALATINAT							
Sachsen-Meiningeh	Carmine	Green	Green	Green	Carmine	Grey	Black tricorn edged white. Tin buttons. Drummer in reverse colours. Officers' sash silver.
Rehbinder, 1707 Coppe	Indigo Blue	Carmine	Carmine	Carmine	Blue	Grey/white	Black tricorn edged yellow. Grenadier hat red front, blue bag, white border. Drummer in reverse colours.
Barbo, 1708 La Marck	Deep Blue	Orange	Orange	Orange	Orange	Grey/white	Black tricorn edged yellow. Yellow buttons Grenadier cap orange front, blue bag, white border and piping. Blue grenade on front bottom. Drummer in reverse colours.
Greber, 1704 Efferen	Deep Blue	Yellow	Yellow	Deep Blue	Leather	Grey	Black tricorn edged yellow. Yellow buttons Drummer in reverse colours with blue and white lace.
Leibregiment, 1707 Aubach	Royal Blue	Royal Blue	Royal Blue	Royal Blue	Royal Blue	Grey/White	Black tricorn edged white. Copper buttons White lace on edge of coat and cuffs and on buttons and button holes.
Garde Grenadiers	Indigo Blue	Red	Red	Red	Blue	Grey/white	Grenadier cap red front, blue bag crest and bomb on front white. Copper buttons. Drummers' and officers' coat red with blue cuffs.
RHINE SUPERIOR							
Hessen Darmstadt	Deep Blue	White	White	White	Deep Blue	Deep Blue	Black tricorn edged white. White lace and buttons and lace across crest of jacket, w/coat and cuffs. Red cravat. Grenadier cap white front with lion rampant, red and white horizontal stripes, blue bag.
Nassau-Weilburg	Deep	White	White	White	White	Grey	Black tricorn edged white. Copper buttons and white cravat. Grenadier cap front blue, yellow grenade, white bag.
Nassau-Weilburg, Frankfurter Kontingent	Deep	Red	Red	Red	Red	Grey	Black tricorn edged white. Copper buttons.
SWABIA							
Rodt	Grey/white	Grey/white	Sky blue	Sky blue	Sky blue	Sky blue	Black tricorn edged white with green foliage. Drummers in reverse colours.
WESTPHALIA							
Uffling	Grey	Yellow	Yellow	Yellow	Grey	White	Black tricorn with yellow lace, green foliage. Drummers in reverse colours. Officers' lace gold.
WURTTEMBERG							
Leibregiment	Grey	Yellow	Yellow	Red	Leather	Grey	Black tricorn edged yellow, green foliage Grenadier cap black front with yellow piping. Yellow bag black tassel. Drummers in reverse colours.
WURZBURG							
Eyb	Grey	Green	Green	Green	Leather	Grey	Black tricorn edged white with green foliage. White buttons and cravat. Drummers in reverse colours.

FLAGS, COLOURS AND STANDARDS

In this short section it would be impossible to provide more than a flavour of the flags, colours and standards of the armies. They represent a most colourful and varied aspect of the period, not least because while a degree of uniformity was slowly being introduced into armies, the personal involvement of the regimental commander provided a considerable influence when it came to the design of flags, colours and standards.

Austria

At the start of the war, every company in an infantry unit carried a flag, the colonel's company a white one and the rest of the regimental facing colour. The flags were approximately 2.20 to almost 3 metres square, with a 20 or 30 cm border. The double eagle borne on them was not embroidered as on the standards of the cavalry, but cut out of the doubled ground cloth and under laid in black cloth, which was sewn into it. The eagle's beak and claws, sceptre, crown, halos and sword handles and the other devices were yellow or golden, the blade of the sword was silver. The eagle appeared in mirror image on the other side of the colour. The flag was wrapped around the larch wood pole, reinforced with cloth bands and held with three rows of about 25 nails. After 1711 there was only one flag per battalion apart from the colonel's battalion, which had two including the colonel's own flag or *leibfahne*.

In all the mounted regiments, each company had its own flag. The cuirassier standards were square, with sides measuring about 480mm, or 18 inches. They mostly had fringes and tassels. The dragoon flags were swallow-tailed guidons, about the same in depth and measured about 700mm from the points of the guidon to the flag staff. In each regiment, the colonel's, or *Leibsquadron* flag, was white. On one side were the arms of Austria, a red and white horizontally striped shield, supported by the black, double headed Imperial eagle. This carried a sword and sceptre. Above the eagle was the Imperial crown and two scrolls. The reverse of the flag carried the colonel's arms or the Virgin and Child emblem. The initials of the colonel, heraldic designs of various types and scrollwork or wreaths often accompanied these designs. Unlike those of the infantry these were embroidered. The other flags were usually coloured but had the same pattern as the colonel's.

Bavaria

The Bavarian infantry carried a colour for each company. The first carried the *leibfahne* (sovereign's colour), which was white with the "gott's mutter" (Virgin and Child) device. The remaining colours were generally geometric pattern of blue and white diamonds resembling cross-hatching.

Cavalry standards were rectangular and like those of the infantry were generally geometric patters of blue and white.

Britain

British foot regiments of the period carried two colours, The first was the colonel's; a plain colour field chosen by the colonel, not necessarily the same as the facing colour, emblazoned with a device chosen by him. The second colour was the based on the St. George's cross. The St. Andrews cross (a white saltire on a blue field) was added after the Act of Union (1707). A similar small union flag was also added in the upper corner of the colonel's nearest the pike.

The cavalry and dragoons carried a mix of standards and guidons. These were made of heavy damask heavily embroidered in gold and silver. There may have been standards or guidons for each troop although, like those of other countries this was reduced and one reads of a number of regiments having just three per regiment.

Danish

Each of the six companies of a Danish infantry regiments possessed its own colour although they may not all have been carried into battle. The Leib, or regimental colour, together with that of the lieutenant colonel's or the major's company would almost certainly have been carried. The Leib colour of most of the regiments may well have been white. The basic infantry colour was about five feet square with no fringes. They were made from a single thickness of silk, which was painted on both sides. Most had, in the upper corner nearest the staff, a small canton containing the dannebrogge, the Danish national emblem, a white cross on a red field. This canton was about a foot square. Each unit would have its own individual patterns on the main field of the colour.

The cavalry standards were of a uniform type. They had a canton about six inches square in the upper corner nearest the staff bearing the *dannebrogge*. The edges were fringed in gold or silver. In the centre was the royal cypher surrounded by a wreath, both in gold. The cavalry standards were about two feet square. They were made from silk damask and were formed by sewing together two lined and embroidered pieces. As a result they were quite stiff and did not flutter as much as the infantry colours.

Dutch

The colonel's, lieutenant colonel's and the major's colours were usually carried in the field reducing to two as the period went on. The colonel's colour was often white, decorated with his coat of arms; the second colour would have had the same pattern but on a different coloured background. In the top corner, nearest the staff, were the arms of the province that maintained the regiment. The colour was about six feet square, carried on a 10 feet long staff with a pike head.

Regiments of cavalry had rectangular standards while dragoons had a guidon with one curved point.

France

The French infantry battalions had a colonel's colour and a regimental or *ordonnance* colour. A battalion carried two or even three of the latter. The colonel's colour was white with a white cross. The Regimental or "ordonnance" colours also had a white cross but with the distinctive quadrant colours to signify the regiment. This could be as simple as all four quadrants being the same colour to varying colours and patterns within each quadrant.

The order of 1 February 1684 required the French cavalry to carry two standards per squadron and the dragoons a similar number of guidons. The cavalry standards were square, between 50 and 60cms across while the dragoon guidons ended in two rounded points and were 80 to 100 cms high and 95 to 125 cms long.

Prussia

The Prussian infantry had *leibfahne* (sovereign's colour) and a regimental colour per company. The design was that which would dominate Prussian flags for the next century with a plain field decorated with a central eagle crest and crowned cyphers in the four corners.

MARLBOROUGH BIBLIOGRAPHY

- Atkinson CT. *Marlborough and the Rise of the British Army*. London 1924.
- Barnett C., *A History of the British Army*; London 1970.
- Barnett C., *Marlborough* 1974.
- Barthorp M., *British Infantry Uniforms since 1660*; 1982.
- Barthorp M., *British Cavalry Uniforms since 1660*; 1984.
- Barthorp M & McBride A. *Marlborough's Army* - Osprey
- Belloc, H., *The Tactics and Strategy of the Great Duke Marlborough*. London 1933.
- Carman, W. Y., *British Military Uniforms from Contemporary Pictures*. 1968.
- Chandler D. *Art of Warfare in the Age of Marlborough* - Spellmount Publishing
- Chandler D., *Blenheim Preparation* - Spellmount Publishing 2004
- Chandler D (ed). *Military Memoirs of Marlborough's Campaigns* - Greenhill Books
- Chandler D. *Marlborough as a Military Commander* - Spellmount Publishing
- Chartand R & Back F. *Louis XIV'Army* - Osprey
- Childs J., *Armies and Warfare In Europe 1648-1789*. 1982.
- Churchill W S. *Marlborough, His Life and Times* - George G Harrap & Co Ltd
- Colonie, M de la. *Chronicles of an Old Campaigner*
- Fortescue, Hon JW. *History of the British Army, Vol 1*
- Fosten D.S., *Blenheim*. 1975.
- Four P., *Trouphees de la Guerre De Succession D'espagne 1700-1713*. 1982.
- Funken L. And F., *The Lace Wars*. 2 Vols. 1977.
- Grant CS. *From Pike to Shot* - Wargames Research Group
- Green D., *Blenheim*. 1974.
- Goldberg And W Agner. *Bema1uagsangaben Fur Die Zeit Des Spanischen Erbflgekrieges 1701-1714*
  (300 Cards Ofb/W Line Drawings Of Uniforms) Hanover - Linden.
- Hall, R. *Flags and Uniforms of the French Infantry under Louis XIV, 1688-1714*.
  The Pike and Shot Society 2002.
- Henderson N. *Prince Eugene of Savoy*
- Hoffmann. *Das Hee.R Des B1auen Konigs*. 1967 (Facsimile).
- Job, Tenues *Des Troupes De France a Toutes 1es Epoques*. 1900-1904.
- Kannik P., *Military Uniforms in Colour*. 1968.
- Kearsey Lt. Col. A., *Marlborough and his Campaigns 1702-1708*. 1960.
- Kemp S. *Weapons and Equipment of the Marlborough Wars* - Blandford 1980
- Knotel R. and H. and Seig H., *Uniforms of the World*. 1980.
- Lawson C.C.P., *A History of Modern Warfare 1618-1815*. 1981.
- Llenhart & Humbert. *Les Uniforms de L'armee Francaise 1690-1894*. 4 Vol. 1897-99.
- Maccarthy Col. M.D. *Soldat du Roi les Armees de L'ancien Regime*. 1984.
- Ottenfeld And Teuber. *Die Osterreichische Armee von 1700 Bis 1867*. Ken Trotman reprint 2004. ≈ 7
- Rogers H.C.B., *The British Army of the 18th Century*. 1977.
- Rothenberg G.E., *The Army of Francis Joseph*. USA, Indiana 1976.
- Scouller Re., *The Armies of Queen Anne*. Oxford 1966.
- Simkin R. *Uniforms of the British Army. The Infantry Regiments*.
- Simkin R. *Uniforms of the British Army. The Cavalry Regiments*. 1982.
- Susane La Vv., *Histoire De L'infanterie Francaise*. 5 Vols. 1876/77.
- Susane Lavv. *Histoire De L'artillerie Francaise*. Paris 1874.
- Susane Lavv. *Histoire De La Cavalerie Francaise*. 1874.
- Susane Lavv. *Histoire De L'ancienne Infanterie Francaise*. Paris. 1849.
- Wace A., *The Marlborough Tapestries at Blenheim Palace*. 1968.
- Walton C., *The History of the British Standing Army 1660-1700*.1894.
- Weygand General, *L'armee Francaise, Paris*. 1938.
- Wilson P., *The Uniforms of Marlborough's Wars*. 1970.

Published Works, Journals and Periodicals

A Number of Manuscripts and Private Collections were consulted in he course of research. Two that contributed significantly were as follows:

The Reynolds Collection (Manuscript Volumes on Uniforms of the British Army (Victoria and Albert Museum).

Uniform plates by Rousselot, Leliepvre and Knotel.
Manuscripts of the Marquess Of Cambridge (National Army Museum).

Of the many journals and periodicals used the following were of particular value:
Campaigns, Gazette Des Uniforms, Journal of the Society for Army Historical Research, La Sabretache; Journal de la Societe des Collection News. De Figurines Historiques, Military Modelling, Tradition.

Editions Brokaw. Various booklets on the Armies of the War of the Spanish Succession